ADVANCE PRAISE FOR *PHOENIX REVIVAL*

"*Phoenix Revival* by Kegan Gill is an inspiring memoir that recounts Gill's remarkable journey from surviving the fastest ejection in naval aviation history to becoming an advocate for alternative medicine and recovery. After ejecting at a speed of 695 mph, Gill suffered severe injuries, including a traumatic brain injury (TBI) and post-traumatic stress disorder (PTSD). His story isn't just about physical recovery; it's also about overcoming addiction, finding alternative healing methods, and ultimately thriving through ultra-endurance sports and public speaking.

Gill's experience with the limitations of conventional treatments for TBI and PTSD led him to explore alternative therapies, including indigenous medicine. His commitment to recovery and wellness turned him into an advocate for others struggling with chronic health conditions, especially veterans. He now shares his story to inspire resilience and holistic approaches to healing.

Gill's journey, documented in *Phoenix Revival*, serves as a testament to the power of the human spirit to overcome adversity through both traditional and alternative methods of healing, making it a must-read for those interested in recovery from trauma and brain injuries."

—**Mark L. Gordon**, MD,
founder of Millennium Health Centers,
a veteran TBI program

"As a fellow veteran, I've seen resilience in many forms, but Kegan Gill's story is truly extraordinary. After ejecting from a jet at dangerous speeds, he faced injuries so severe that doctors said he would never walk again. Yet, through sheer determination, he defied those odds and conquered obstacle after obstacle along the way. I had the honor of meeting him during an ultramarathon, where his perseverance and unyielding warrior spirit were on full display. His journey is an inspiring testament to the power of the human will, and this book will motivate anyone who reads it to face life's challenges head-on. An unforgettable story of courage, strength, and unwavering resolve."

—**Jesse Gould,**
former US Army Ranger,
founder of Heroic Hearts Project

"As a former SEAL and a physician for thousands of SEALs, I have had the good fortune to work with some of the most amazing survivors in the world. However, nothing comes close to Kegan's story. His story is the most impactful and amazing tale of survival and determination I have ever heard, and Kegan's humility and humor make the story even more amazing and enjoyable. Do yourself the favor of reading this amazing adventure. I know you will find inspiration beyond what you previously thought possible."

—**Kirk R. Parsley**, MD, former US Navy SEAL

"The durability of a man is a direct reflection of his life and the experiences he has had. In the harshest moments of life, durability is the one quality that cannot be absent. It is the ability to withstand wear, pressure, or damage. In Kegan's story, you will find his ability to overcome extreme obstacles is not a result of resources or talent but rather an innate drive to survive. He truly is one of the most durable humans I know, and I'm honored to be part of his journey."

—**Justin Sheehan**, US Navy SEAL

"I could not stop reading this book once I started it. SMURF's story is a cookbook of turning lemons into lemonade. Reading his account of the aftermath of his ejection brought with it a flood of memories surrounding that time in our professional and personal lives together in the Dogs. Being young and naive, I thought we were all invincible. Little did any of us know that the ejection over Mary Lee's hunting ground was only the beginning of a half-decade long nightmare that he had to pull himself out of, much like a nose-low maneuver in the G Bucket. Kegan's grit, unending optimism, and support of his family are a true testament to the indomitable nature of the human spirit and demonstrate that we nailed his call sign—he is one Scrappy MotherFucker, a.k.a. SMURF."

—**LCDR Tom "FISTY" Flynn,**
US Navy F/A-18 pilot

"In life, we often encounter defining moments—those times when the world seems to either break us down or force us to rise in ways we never thought possible. Survival and resiliency are words that carry immense weight, especially to those who've stood at the edge and been tested by fire. I've seen firsthand how the human spirit can transcend the harshest trials. That's why Kegan Gill's insights into survival and resilience resonate so profoundly with me. He has distilled a lifetime of wisdom into these pages, hard-won lessons that only come from pushing through limits and defying odds.

Kegan isn't just writing from a place of theory. He's been through his own crucibles, faced down physical and mental challenges, and emerged with a strength few can claim. His insights here aren't simply lessons; they're lifelines. As a fellow veteran, I know what it's like to wrestle with the demands of the body and mind under pressure. It's a fight that calls on every ounce of fortitude, demanding endurance in ways we can only understand in hindsight. Kegan's work stands as both a guide and a testament for anyone seeking to cultivate resilience, whether facing physical trials, mental strains, or simply the day-to-day struggles that come from walking an uncommon path.

In these pages of *Phoenix Revival*, you won't just find strategies for survival; you'll find a roadmap to strength—an invitation to tap into reserves of courage you may not even know you have.

Kegan has walked the walk. This book is a bridge between his experiences and the strength within each of us. I'm honored to call him a friend and proud to introduce his work to you. Prepare to be challenged, inspired, and transformed."

—**Christian Meyers,**
founder of Terra Arma, cohost of *The MEDEVAC Podcast*

"The story of Kegan Gill is not just one of survival but of extraordinary resilience. Surviving the harrowing ejection from a jet—an event that most can hardly imagine—Kegan faced the immediate, life-altering physical and mental toll. Yet, it was his journey of recovery that tells the deeper story, one that highlights the relentless preservation of self and the unyielding strength of family.

Through unimaginable pain, both physical and emotional, Kegan's spirit and determination emerged as a beacon of hope. His resilience serves as a reminder of what the human will is capable of enduring and overcoming. He fought not just to heal his body but to rebuild his life, to be present for his loved ones, and to reclaim his purpose. His story is one of inspiration for anyone facing adversity, showing that the path forward may be challenging but never impossible.

However, Kegan's experience also uncovers a profound truth that cannot be ignored: The VA system, meant to serve our bravest men and women, often falls tragically short. The treatment he and others like him received reveals the systemic failures that must be urgently addressed. Veterans deserve more—they deserve the best care, not just after traumatic events but throughout their healing journey.

Kegan's story is a call to action. It's time for a thorough review and reform of the VA system so that every veteran receives the treatment, respect, and attention they have earned through their service and sacrifice."

—**SGM Harold Hill,**
US Army (Ret.), US Army Special Operations

"Kegan's journey to becoming a navy F/A-18E pilot was a heroic endeavor. His near-fatal ejection and fight to get back into the cockpit exemplify the strength of the human spirit that few will ever know. The unexpected fight for his life came as he navigated the VA mental health care system for his post-traumatic stress and traumatic brain injury, a system beholden to Big Pharma rather than the complete, comprehensive care of veterans. Kegan fought fiercely for his life and won. His diligence in seeking healing rather than medications has given him his life back and a new purpose in championing change for veterans' mental health care."

—Donna Cranston,
founder & CEO of Defenders of Freedom

"I've had the privilege of witnessing Kegan Gill's remarkable journey firsthand, and his autobiography is a testament to his resilience, determination, and inspiring spirit. This candid and reflective memoir offers a rare glimpse into the life of a truly extraordinary son, husband, father, and sailor!"

—Dr. Scharlene Gaudet, DC, MSc, DACNB,
founder of Resiliency Brain Health

"If you are facing challenges and need inspiration to move past them, this is the book for you. Kegan redefines his challenges into opportunities for growth. He is by far one of the most impressive people I have ever met. He is the perfect combination of steadfast, disciplined, kind, and motivated. We can all take a page from his book and apply it to our own lives. He is the definition of resiliency."

—Dr. Michelle Eisenmann, DC, MSc, DACNB,
Resiliency Brain Health

"In fifteen years of working with our nation's warriors through Operation Surf, I've heard countless stories of resilience, but none like Kegan's. Kegan's story is a powerful reminder of what's possible. Sticking your hand out of a car window at 60 mph is already significant—being ejected from an F/A-18E at 695 mph? It's beyond comprehension. His determination to heal after his tremendous accident and to fly again, even after another flight malfunction, speaks to the heart of what it means to persevere.

It was a privilege to take Kegan surfing and watch him rise again, mentally and physically. His strength, courage, and ability to find hope in the darkest moments show us that even when the battle feels endless, the journey is worth it. His ability to choose himself didn't just benefit him; it positively affected his family, his community, and even me.

Kegan's survival defies belief, showing the incredible power of human perseverance. His unwavering spirit is a testament to his identity as a true warrior."

—Van Curaza,
professional big wave surfer, founder of Operation Surf

"Kegan and I met over a piece of wood.

Before that, he had been my wife's patient in physical therapy and part of the fighter pilot community, which was forced on me through her work friends and patient demographic on the naval air base.

He told me he was familiar with force reconnaissance corpsmen; I tried to correct him, saying, 'I doubt it' since there are only about 150 in the navy. He explained he'd taken some long dive chamber rides with one of my peers, who was indeed a good friend. I think that's when the extent of the damage that had been done to his body dawned on me, hyperbaric tissue healing being reserved for the worst cases. Despite what he was going through—the incredible recovery I was witnessing—Kegan showed tremendous respect for me, his healers, and his peers. There was gratitude on his sleeve. Not all people are like this in recovery.

Back to the wood. I was meeting up with him and others to surf one day and knew that he was on his way to getting married. I can't recall why, but I felt I needed to give him a gift. Being into woodworking at the time, I impulsively decided he should have a piece of Indian rosewood I had acquired overseas. Once at the beach, I handed him his gift, receiving curious looks from all. Kegan was not a woodworker. I left the beach that day, unsure why I had given him that gift.

I had gotten into woodworking a year or two before meeting Kegan. Another reconnaissance corpsman, Dan Brown, had explained that the small repetitive movements and details I was working on with my chisels were healing my brain. Dan had been healing from a combat-related brain injury at the time, and he'd told me I was healing myself without knowing it, that I liked woodworking because I needed it. *Perhaps*, I'd thought.

When I gave Kegan that gift, he had just been surfing. He was all lean muscle, and he was taking some orders to continue being a fighter pilot; his recovery was over. But, as the cliché goes, not all wounds are visible.

I later received a gorgeously turned tobacco pipe crafted by him out of that same rosewood, and I was privy to many beautiful works that followed.

My friend Dan might have had some good years ahead of him, but he decided to leave this world on his own terms. Next month, I will attend a celebration of life for Joey, another peer whose wounds went unnoticed.

This book is essential. Mental scar tissue seems invisible to others and is often denied by oneself. Even if it rips open anew, we deny it and try to seal it back up, lest those demons leak out. When we hear about this struggle from others, we can turn toward it, see it, and work less alone."

—**Leo Perez**, SARC, US Navy Special Warfare

"Kegan 'SMURF' Gill's life changed forever when he was ejected from his F/A-18E at supersonic speed. His body shattered upon impact, yet his unwavering spirit kept him afloat in the ocean for hours, refusing to give up.

Kegan's determination to return to the cockpit drove him to push through the pain, enduring multiple surgeries and grueling physical therapy sessions. But the true battle lay in healing the invisible wounds: a traumatic brain injury and PTSD.

'I realized that modern medicine could only take me so far,' Kegan says. 'To truly heal, I needed a community that understood my experiences and shared my passion for recovery.'

Kegan found that community among fellow survivors, and together, they discovered the courage to overcome their challenges and inspire others to rise again. Kegan's story of resilience and community inspired me to seek out my own healing journey, reminding me that with courage and support, we can overcome even the toughest obstacles."

—LTC Herb Daniels,
US Army Special Forces

"Sometimes in life, we feel like we're in a nose-low dive toward a catastrophic crash—a metaphor for hitting rock bottom. For Kegan Gill, an F/A-18E fighter pilot, this was no metaphor; it became his reality on January 15, 2014. After surviving the fastest ejection in naval aviation history, literally bouncing off the sound barrier, Kegan had no idea his toughest battle was yet to come. The military medical system, intended to heal, would ultimately do more harm to his physical, mental, and emotional health than that harrowing escape ever could.

But Kegan is a once-in-a generation leader who refused to be defeated by the system or his circumstances. He fought through unimaginable pain, psychosis, and betrayal from a healthcare system meant to protect him and emerged as a beacon of hope for those trapped in their own struggles.

Kegan's story is not just one of survival; it's a guide for anyone who feels like they're spiraling out of control, proving that no matter how deep the dive, you can always pull up, find your strength, find your tribe, find your purpose, and soar again. This book will inspire you to take the first step toward healing and break free from the darkness."

—**Adam Marr**, "GHOSTRIDER 6," US Army AH-64D/E Apache pilot, director of operations at Veteran Mental Health Leadership Coalition, cohost of The American Legion's *Tango Alpha Lima Podcast*

"'Be who you are and be that well.' This quote by St. Francis de Sales from four centuries ago gives direct insight into the story of my friend Kegan Gill, recounted through his transformative book *Phoenix Revival*.

Kegan's story is one of legend, and it parallels the myth of the flying phoenix as an autobiography of destruction and rebirth. The story of the phoenix is one told throughout humankind and one that we all share the potential to experience in both the lowest and highest moments of humanity. However, on first pass, one may only see the surface of the story as physical instead of a story of spirit. The physical side of the story is one of a pilot who experiences to a tragic accident in which a computer malfunction steals the capacity for pilot override and leads to the destruction of both a US Navy fighter jet and the human pilot. This story, in mythical fashion, is one of recovery from fiery destruction and the rising from adversity as a rebirth. However, this is only a partial representation of the true mythology of the phoenix and the US Navy fighter pilot found within this story. The physical destruction of the human corpus with battered flail limbs, neuropraxia, saltwater lungs, hypothermal and hypovolemic shock, and a traumatic brain injury (TBI) is one story of the physical insult that doctors and surgeons as well as the reader can find in these pages. This story is well known in treatise, medical reports, and poetry, as it is the iterative physical story of the phoenix told and experienced by generations of human struggle. And like any myth, there is always a far deeper story to be interpreted and then used to inform the subconscious. The rebirth story that on the surface seems to be physical for both LT Gill and the phoenix is only a sliver of the story. The true story of Kegan Gill and the phoenix through history has always been a story of the spirit and soul going through rebirth.

As a craniofacial plastic surgeon who has treated countless children born with the most complex congenital and acquired conditions, I have seen and been the architect of physical rebirth. I was the only craniofacial surgeon on the Boston face transplant team that performed more face transplants than any other team in the world. And some of those patients similarly went through a physical rebirth, like Kegan and the phoenix. However, those stories as told by a successful surgical episode, in many instances, were often only the start of the healing quest. Healing is not physical. In truth, healing must be an encounter with consciousness and the spirit.

The true or deeper story here in these pages is one of physical rebirth with a heroic rescue and lifesaving trauma care, followed by the epic failure of the health system to not care for the TBI and mental side of healing. This story and the telling of it is a testament to the fact that Kegan Gill is one of the most resilient men I have ever met. Recounted here is the story of his mental rebirth, and it can be one of inspiration for conscientious readers. I know his story through the personal blessing of meeting this man during his journey back from the state of mental anguish. His story of being the phoenix incarnate is one that will inspire you to introspectively evaluate your own path and soul. Kegan Gill is a father, a husband, and my friend. And like the insight written four hundred years ago, he lives a life of love, emulating the advice to be who you are and to be that well."

—**E.J. Caterson**, MD, PhD, surgeon

"*Phoenix Revival* is more than just a memoir; it's a beacon of hope and resilience for anyone facing unmatched challenges. Lieutenant Kegan 'SMURF' Gill's story is an extraordinary testament to the power of the human spirit. From a near-fatal ejection at supersonic speed to an inspiring return to the skies, Lieutenant Gill's narrative is one of determination and sheer willpower. I am proud to call SMURF a friend and even prouder to have read his story."

—Kelsi Sheren,
CEO of Brass & Unity, author, and host

"This book tells the secret of the biggest tragedy in the largest healthcare system in the world. Americans like Kegan are chewed up and spit out every minute of every day, and there has to be something done about it. Learn about the truth behind the VA.

Getting to know Kegan was one of the best things in my life. He is a true American hero, a genuine friend, father, and husband. When you hear his story, you realize that your troubles in life aren't so big. Be prepared for inspiration.

I had the opportunity to meet Kegan on his journey to sleep restoration. I found more than just an incredible human being who has encountered more suffering than most people hear stories about. Watching his perseverance and success despite all excuses is truly inspiring. I hope you enjoy his story."

—Robert Sweetman,
former US Navy SEAL, sleep genius,
and founder of 62Romeo

"*I nearly killed my friend.*
In naval aviation, any time there is an unexpected or undesirable outcome, we collaborate to understand what happened, why, and how to be better next time. We call this the debrief. Accountability in the debrief is the mark of the most professional among us. Being critical, first, of ourselves. Our decisions. Our actions. Did we choose right? Did we execute correctly? And, if our first

notes in the debrief are not about where we failed and where we could be better next time, we're wrong.

Those among us who shirk this responsibility and accountability are known. Known as phonies, liabilities, or worse. If you pay close attention to this book, you'll notice that Kegan takes ALL the blame for the sequence of events that left him floating in the ice-cold Atlantic Ocean on January 15, 2014. Floating in a shredded dry suit, with exposed fractures to every extremity . . . the least severe of his injuries. Pay close attention, and you'll notice that he is a true professional. He identifies and takes responsibility for his errors in decision-making and execution. And that is where it stops. Could he have made better decisions? Could he have executed better? Could he have been in a more controlled setting where he could not have even 'gotten there' in the first place? Yes. Yes. And yes. And you would never know it by hearing only his account, but he bears none of the responsibility for being on that flight, airborne in a nonstandard and unfamiliar setting.

His decisions and execution? Well, you'll have to read his account for yourself, but while he was in the airplane by himself, he was not alone. His training, and that of the rest of the squadron, were my direct responsibility. And quite simply, looking at this accident with the sobriety it deserves, I failed. There is an old quote, unattributed to anyone in particular as far as I know, that goes like this: 'Whenever we talk about a pilot who has been killed in a flying accident, we should all keep one thing in mind. He called upon the sum of all his knowledge and made a judgment. He believed it so strongly that he knowingly bet his life on it. That his judgment was faulty was a tragedy, not stupidity. Every inspector, supervisor, and contemporary who ever spoke to him had an opportunity to influence his judgment, so a little of all of us goes with every pilot we lose.'

Well, thank God that we didn't lose SMURF in a flying accident, but it got pretty damn close. And not only did I have an 'opportunity' to influence his judgment, I had a responsibility to. And any mistake he may have made that day is on me. And our skipper. And our operations officer. And our scheduling officer. And his instructors in the RAG . . . And . . . And . . . And as the quote's author says, anyone with the 'opportunity to influence his judgment.' And that is just it—he is not the only human whose mistakes nearly killed him that day. But he is the only human standing tall and taking accountability for them. What an outstanding man. And that accident is only the first act in his remarkable story. An act that surely would have taken the weaker among us and rendered us victims of our circumstances. Not in the case of my friend, Kegan 'SMURF' Gill, a seeming superhuman, whose descent into the depths of physical, mental, and emotional hellfire has only forged him into a stronger human. Reborn, like the phoenix of legend, into the incredible human he is today: father, husband, and tireless activist for those less capable."

—**CDR Scott "CAWK" Golich,**
US Navy Reserve, F/A-18 pilot

"Kegan Gill is my kind of hero. He endured unthinkable disaster and adversity, but rather than allowing his past to consume him, he took the path of service—higher than any jet can fly."

—**Eric "MOOSE" Smith,** former US Navy SEAL

"Kegan's harrowing tale of surviving the incredible ordeal of ejecting from a navy fighter jet is riveting, but it is his journey of overcoming the trauma and adversity that followed that truly sets his story apart. His transformation from a place of brokenness to one of health, productivity, and resilience is nothing short of awe-inspiring. Through his raw and honest storytelling, Kegan offers a compelling narrative of hope, courage, and the power of the human spirit to triumph over even the most daunting challenges. This book is a must-read for anyone seeking inspiration and a testament to the incredible strength we all possess to overcome adversity in spite of overwhelming circumstances."

—**LtCol Dave Deep,**
USMC (Ret.), former Apache Pilot,
founder of Wake for Warriors

"Kegan Gill is a testament to the resilience of the human spirit. After barely surviving the fastest successful ejection from a fighter aircraft, Kegan's journey of courage and determination saw him not only return to the cockpit but also overcome a traumatic brain injury (TBI) that emerged years later. I had the privilege of witnessing his transformation firsthand while sprinting alongside him on an ice-carved runway in Antarctica. Watching him outpace me with a backpack and heavy boots was awe-inspiring.

Kegan's journey infuses *Phoenix Revival* with a powerful authenticity that speaks to the spirit of overcoming life's greatest challenges. His firsthand experiences of resilience and rebirth offer a deeply moving and inspiring perspective. This book is more than a story—it's a reflection of what we are capable of when we refuse to give up. *Phoenix Revival* is a must-read for anyone seeking inspiration and courage."

—LTC Chris "ROBIE" Robishaw,
US Army Special Forces (Ret.),
founder of Tip of the Spear Landmine Removal

"Kegan Gill's spirit manifests the warrior's indomitable drive for adventure and excellence. His tale of rising to the heights of naval aviation as an F/A-18E Super Hornet pilot and then pulling himself out of the depths of despair after ejecting at the Mach is a must-read story that lays bare the heart of a warrior.

Phoenix Revival is a fast-paced and hard-hitting read. Many of us would have 'punched out' of life altogether when facing the daunting aftermath of an ejection into the cold waters of the Atlantic while inverted and accelerating at 650 knots. Ripped apart physically, psychologically, and spiritually, Kegan's journey home is a tale of hardship and grit that sends shivers through the spine. His exit on the backside as a beacon of strength to other warriors surviving trauma and the battering of an overwhelmed VA care system gives hope to those of us watching from the sidelines."

—Mark "WILLY" Williams,
former US Air Force F-15C pilot, cofounder of The Wisdom Dojo

"This is a story based on the fundamental, unfathomable will of human potential, beyond the physical body and the physical brain, in some unknown recess of the mind that drives us forward to the impossible. It makes me proud to be a human being."

—**William Filter**,
master meditation coach,
cofounder of The Wisdom Dojo

PHOENIX REVIVAL
THE AFTERMATH OF NAVAL AVIATION'S FASTEST SURVIVED EJECTION

LT Kegan "Smurf" Gill USN (Ret.)

Ballast Books, LLC
www.ballastbooks.com

Copyright © 2025 by Kegan Gill

ISBN: 978-1-964934-51-8 (hardcover)
978-1-964934-52-5 (paperback)
978-1-964934-57-0 (ebook)

Printed in the United States of America

Published by Ballast Books
www.ballastbooks.com

For more information, bulk orders, appearances, or speaking requests, please email: info@ballastbooks.com

To all those who feel trapped in darkness: You are not alone. This is for you. There is light, even when it seems impossible to find.

INTRODUCTION

Nothing in my rigorous training as a naval strike fighter pilot could have prepared me for the invisible, silent battle I was about to face. While my squadron mates fought overseas, I was in a different life-threatening fight. This is a battle not fought in distant lands but right here on the home front, within the minds and hearts of millions of Americans.

According to health institutions like the National Institute of Mental Health, the *Journal of the American Medical Association*, and the Centers for Disease Control and Prevention, about 50 percent of the US population will grapple with some form of mental health challenges during their lifetime. That's a coin toss determining whether you or someone close to you might be thrown into this unseen war.

Despite its prevalence, our country's current approach to health care often falls painfully short. With shockingly low success rates, traditional treatments frequently worsen the very issues they aim to solve, leaving millions to suffer in silence, their conditions exacerbated by the treatments meant to help them.

I am one of the lucky ones. Perhaps I am even the luckiest man alive. I survived what many have not, with my mental faculties intact. My journey through the depths of a failing health system and back again has instilled in me a new mission: to share a remarkable true story that not only captivates but also illuminates the path for others battling these often invisible

foes. This book is not an indictment of the medical professionals who work tirelessly to aid us but a critique of the system and
established industry that binds their hands.

Join me as I recount a personal survival, resilience, and transformational saga. This is more than my memoir; it's a rallying
cry for change and a guide to reclaiming our health, empower-
ing you to navigate your wellness with courage and hope. Strap
in and prepare for a journey through the highs and lows of my
life. It's a unique flight through adversity that's unlike anything
you've ever encountered.

CHAPTER 1

January 15, 2014: My eyes were bloodshot, punished by hours of intense focus on a laptop screen as I programmed a stack of thumb drive–like mission cards for the upcoming air wing large force exercise (LFE). The stuffy, windowless room was packed with highly caffeinated, seasoned, and aggressive Type A personalities. Besides the sadistic weapon system officer, who was orchestrating the rigorous, week-long mission planning phase, we would have much rather been in the cockpit.

The self-escort strike we were designing served as preparation for the hazardous task of launching dozens of our air wing's aircraft simultaneously into shared airspace to train for complex air-to-air warfare. Despite its chaotic nature, training as close to the real thing as possible prepared us to handle the worst-case scenarios that could arise.

Executing an LFE self-escort strike requires aircrew to utilize the wide range of skills the F/A-18 is designed for. In the event of actual warfare, a single aircraft carrier can mobilize an entire air wing, enabling us to penetrate enemy lines and strike strategic targets almost anywhere in the world. This capability positions the aircraft carrier as a powerful game changer in the grand scheme of global geopolitics.

As the LFE planning dragged on, I eagerly absconded from the room, the anticipation of the afternoon's flight lighting up my nerves. Upon escaping the steel-and-concrete confines of the Naval Air Station Oceana's TOPGUN Weapons School, the open sky promised an afternoon of thrill.

Engulfing my bagged lunch during the brief transit across the master jet base, I made my way up the narrow hangar staircase into the Strike Fighter Squadron One-Four-Three (also known as the World Famous Pukin' Dogs)–ready room. The VFA-143 duty desk was occupied by Fisty, my good friend and squadron mate, who bore an uncanny resemblance to Chris Pratt in terms of his charm and ability to nail impersonations that boosted morale through our grind.

Humor, especially the kind that teetered on the edge of sanity, was the lifeblood that kept us sane in the high-stakes world of strike-fighter aviation. Case in point: Fisty used a shark tracker app to playfully mark the real-time positions of GPS-tagged sharks on the squadron duty officer's whiteboard. One particular entry, a massive thirty-five hundred pound, sixteen-foot Great White named Mary Lee, lurked ominously below the airspace I was about to occupy. With the water off-shore chilling at a frigid 37 degrees Fahrenheit, Fisty, in his usual wisecracking manner, commented that today would be a less-than-ideal day to eject.

Having served eight months with the squadron, Fisty and I had barely graduated from being the Fuckin' New Guys (FNGs). Nonetheless, every day served a fresh brew of lessons as we guzzled knowledge from the firehose of experience necessary to stay alive. In our squadron, the Pukin' Dogs, the newcomer is anointed with the call sign "Poop," the most worthless part of the dog.

Fisty had only recently earned his call sign after a near mishap that briefly had him on thin ice. He'd inadvertently sailed through an active restricted area that didn't appear on the aircraft's electronic moving map. Technology can be a fickle friend, luring you into a trap without so much as a warning. A few seconds of lousy timing nearly landed him in the unenviable position of being the inadvertent target of a live Stinger heat-seeking missile tested by US Marines to shoot down aircraft. Thus, he was christened Fisty—Flew-Into-Stinger-Territory.

One of the Pukin' Dogs' experienced pilots, Basil, noted that I still needed to do something sufficiently idiotic to earn a call sign. A whiteboard in the ready room served as a leaderboard for the newest pilots, with various potential call signs scribbled next to their names. My list was a rather anemic list of throw-away suggestions. My strategy of keeping my mouth shut and ears open had paid off as I steadily navigated through this maze.

Navy call signs are often badges of dishonor, marking embarrassing blunders committed by the pilots. The more mortifying the incident, the stickier the call sign, especially if it grates on the recipient. Basil's call sign is a prime example, allegedly stemming from an intimate relationship with his sister-in-law. While this is possibly pure fiction, Bangs-A-Sister-In-Law seemed to have a ring, and Basil hated it, so it stuck.

Moments before my flight brief, I did a quick once-over of the briefing room, ensuring that no rogue phallic doodles had appeared on my immaculate briefing board. These sneaky drawings were a popular prank, a whimsical way to keep spirits high and to put those with less attention to detail in the hot seat. The objective was to sketch a small male appendage so subtly that the presenter wouldn't notice until he was knee-deep in a serious briefing in front of an audience of seasoned pilots. I was relieved to see my board was free of such juvenile artistry, and it passed muster as our flight of three pilots went over the day's mission.

The bone-chilling water and sub-freezing air temperatures necessitated wearing dry suits for our sortie over the Atlantic. It had been an exceptionally frigid winter.

Getting ready to pilot a F/A-18E Super Hornet was an experience that bordered on the surreal. At the tender age of twenty-eight, with my cherubic features, I must've looked like Doogie Howser playing dress-up to the grizzled chiefs manning the squadron maintenance department. Despite my boyish countenance making bouncers scrutinize my ID like it was forged, I was about to be handed the reins of an eighty-nine-million-dollar Lot 27 F/A-18E Super Hornet.

The F/A-18E is the Swiss Army knife of fighter jets. It's a single-seat variant armed with a pointy nose, bubble canopy, twin afterburning engines, a sophisticated flight control system, an APG-73 attack radar, and a six-barrel M61A2 Vulcan cannon. It boasts a tailhook and robust landing gear for aircraft carrier landings. This fourth-generation fighter jet is a veritable weapons platform, a jack-of-all-trades, albeit master of none. As I contemplated this, the whisper of imposter syndrome rustled in my mind. Just how did a kid like me wind up in the driver's seat of one of the most advanced warbirds ever built?

Entering the paraloft, a familiar olfactory cocktail greeted me, the heady fusion of jet fuel, well-worn leather, and human musk that pervaded the cramped locker room. Like any pilot worth his salt, I quietly cursed the inconvenience of wriggling into my clammy dry suit. Over this, I zipped up a G suit that bore a passing resemblance to a set of faded green stirrups. When plugged into the cockpit's pressurized air system, the G suit inflates during aggressive maneuvers, helping to force the blood from your legs and core back into your brain, staving off incapacitation via gravity-induced loss of consciousness (G-LOC).

Next came a snug-fitting, full-body parachute harness, soon my lifeline to the ejection seat and parachute. A poorly adjusted harness can lead to profoundly uncomfortable and potentially offspring-compromising situations. I slid my arms into my survival vest, its pockets brimming with relics: a PRC-90 radio, knife, inflatable life preserver (LPU), and an assortment of signaling equipment.

The austere plastic flask we were issued held stale-tasting water, a far cry from the choice spirits once provided to embolden downed pilots. A single swig of the plastic-flavored water could extinguish any lingering will to live. The fun police and bean counters were hell-bent on wringing the fighter spirit out of naval aviation.

Strapping on a pair of brown leather steel-toe boots over the dry suit's booties, I felt a surge of pride. Aviators favor these distinctively brown boots over the black ones worn by surface warfare officers, or SWOs. This tradition dates back to the early days of naval aviation. While the black boots of the SWOs were ideal for camouflaging coal dust from the ships, brown boots were favored by aviators to conceal the dust of the early airfields. More importantly, brown boots irritate SWOs.

Once fully suited up, a squared-away parachute rigger (PR) assisted me with my JHMCS (pronounced jah-HIM-ex) helmet. The Joint Helmet Mounted Cueing System is a marvel of engineering that allows pilots to direct aircraft weapon systems simply by looking around. It uses magnets to track head position, making the weapon systems precisely follow the pilot's gaze. This helmet also displays vital flight information like altitude and airspeed. It's something straight out of a sci-fi movie, and dropping one with a price tag higher than my mortgage is frowned upon.

Stepping out onto the flight line, the bracing winter wind was a welcome refreshment. Even under the cold sky, my dry suit rapidly transformed into a personal sauna, a puddle of sweat pooling under the thirty-five pounds of gear. Despite my ears being cushioned by the foam combat ear protection and my helmet, the omnipresent thunder of jet noise was an inescapable melody, the relentless roar of Super Hornets thrumming through my bones as they prowled around the master jet base.

My mission today called for a hot switch, the hand-off of a jet fresh from a sortie, idling on one engine as it swapped pilots. Through the tinted lens of my JHMCS visor, I sighted Jet 103 with its faded VFA-143 tail markings smoothly cruising down the taxiway. Pulling up to its spot on the VFA-143 flight line, the canopy rose, and my dashingly handsome squadron mate, capable of growing the world's finest mustache, descended the ladder. A cursory salute to the plane captain and a firm handshake assured me the jet was good to go.

Climbing the eight-foot ladder into the cockpit, I began a meticulous once-over of the ejection seat. As the bubble canopy descended, encasing me in my own little world, I started to make the space mine. With careful deliberation, I connected my cords and G suit air hose to the aircraft. One misstep connecting the JHMCS cables could lead to a beheading in an ejection scenario. With each movement measured and purposeful, I navigated through my flowing memorized checklists, ensuring everything was as it should be.

Further rounds of checklists and the other engine was primed for ignition. A flick of the switch and high-pressure air set the left engine, whirring to life as a mix of fuel, air, and sparks ignited the spinning turbines. I closely monitored the RPM and temperature, ensuring no malfunctions were afoot. With both engines humming, I wrapped up my post-start checks, then calibrated my new JHMCS helmet to the jet's internal magnetic system for precise head movement tracking.

Across the flight line, I spotted my good old friend clambering into his VFA-213 Blacklion Super Hornet. It seemed like only yesterday that we were green recruits at Officer Candidate School, enduring the wrath of marine drill instructors as sweat and snot blurred our faces. Spotting me, I greeted him with a good-natured one-finger salute, which he promptly returned.

Today's flight lead was my commanding officer, Diego, a US Navy Fighter Weapons School (TOPGUN) grad and a tactical maestro, having clocked nearly two decades in naval aviation. To me, he was the embodiment of a superhero. I aspired to one day match his level of proficiency to become a seasoned, combat-tested fighter pilot. But for now, my goals were more humble: to hold my position on his wing and sound cool on the radio.

A brief radio check confirmed that everyone was primed and ready to roll. Diego radioed ground for our taxi clearance. Manipulating the dual throttles with my left hand and guiding the rudder pedals with my feet, I maneuvered into position for takeoff beside Diego's jet.

The calm voice of air traffic control crackled over the primary radio. "Taproom three-one and flight cleared for takeoff, runway one zero right."

As Diego's jet shot ahead, I rammed the throttles into maximum afterburner. Forty-four thousand pounds of raw thrust came alive behind me, jet fuel spraying into the heated turbine exhaust and transforming my aircraft into a veritable rocket.

The afterburners punched me back into my seat as the jet hurtled toward rotation speed. With a gentle nudge on the control stick, the plane ascended gracefully into the clear blue sky. The distinct *clunk clunk* of the landing gear retracting prompted me to verify on the indicator lights that the wheels were safely stowed, after which I increased my speed past two hundred and fifty knots to link up in close formation with Diego. Despite the unusually frigid temperatures, the weather was mostly clear, dotted with scattered clouds that provided a scenic backdrop for our sortie.

Upon reaching the W-72 warning area airspace, starting fifty miles off the Virginia Beach coastline, we dove straight into our first task: testing an aerial refueling system (ARS) pod fresh from maintenance. The ARS pod was a large fuel reservoir equipped with a retractable basket, enabling aerial refueling from another Super Hornet. Hipster, ever the embodiment of cool-headed competence, piloted the tanker jet. At the same time, Diego and I assumed positions on his port side, ready to refuel. I extended my fuel probe and ensured my radar and arm switch were off to prevent inadvertently irradiating Hipster with the high-power attack radar housed in my jet's nose. With that, Hipster extended the thick, black fuel hose and basket from his ARS pod, allowing the airflow to stabilize the basket just behind his aircraft.

Positioned right behind Hipster, I cautiously maneuvered my probe into the basket using the subtlest of adjustments to the control stick and throttles. Seeing a green light illuminating the ARS pod was a welcome confirmation of a solid seal. Hipster proceeded to pump fuel into my tanks without a hitch. After a couple more practice plugs to keep our skills sharp, we were ready to transition to high-aspect basic fighter maneuvering (BFM).

Breaking formation with Hipster, Diego and I moved to our designated airspace to hone one of the most exhilarating skills in our repertoire. BFM entails steering a jet at its operational limits to take down another fighter within visual range. It's often likened to a knife fight in a phone booth with an elephant perched on your lap—part physics, part art, part high-intensity interval training. Though it's among the most challenging skills, BFM was my favorite. Like any intricate skill, it called for constant practice to improve. This was my first opportunity to engage in BFM since receiving my JHMCS helmet qualification. I could gain an edge in a dogfight by leveraging the helmet with an array of switches on the throttle and stick (collectively known as HOTAS), but it would take a fair amount of practice before it all became second nature.

Today I was the proverbial beginner, a white belt stepping into the ring with a seasoned and formidable black belt. I knew I was in for a bruising. But this was par for the course in naval aviation—you're thrown into the deep end and left to figure out how to stay afloat.

Once correctly aligned, we announced speed and angels, signaling we were ready to engage. We veered away from each other, carving out a few miles of space before swooping back in like knights in a high-speed jousting match. The miles shrink into nothingness in a matter of seconds at these speeds. As we hurtled past each other at breakneck speed, we each called "Fight's on!" over the tactical radio frequency. From this point on, it was each pilot for himself, each attempting to maneuver his jet to gun down the other before falling prey himself.

BFM is akin to four-dimensional chess, demanding forward thinking at high speed. It's like attempting to weave through heavy traffic at full speed, engage in conversation, and battle a heavyweight simultaneously. The strain on a rookie fighter pilot's brain can be intense enough to induce a so-called "helmet fire."

The resultant g-forces make everything feel nearly eight times heavier when the aircraft is forced into a hard turn. My 180-pound body plus roughly forty pounds of flight gear felt like it weighed a staggering sixteen hundred pounds under seven and a half g's. The g-force is utterly crushing. Due to these intense forces, pilots have been known to suffer from broken necks, backs, or ribs. Despite the assistance of a G suit, high g's force blood away from the brain, potentially causing the pilot to black out in a state known as G-LOC. If not countered with proper breathing and squeezing, this can swiftly lead to a fatal crash.

In the thick of the dogfight, the jets rise, dive, twist, and flip upside down as they dance and weave around each other. I manipulated the throttles and flight controls to gain positional advantage or, at the very least, avoid being shot down. The airframe vibrated as my sleek, gray jet cleaved through the highspeed air. Vapor trails spewed from the flexing wingtips as the surrounding air was torn asunder. Diego's vast experience and expertise soon shone through as he steadily secured a positional upper hand and landed a simulated shot on me.

Diego's confident voice growled, "Fox three," followed quickly by "Knock it off, knock it off." It was clear that Diego decisively won the round with a timely simulated missile shot.

We readied ourselves for several more rounds. As expected, Diego repeatedly bested me. But with each loss, I learned a little more. My body and mind slowly began to work in tandem, transitioning from deliberate actions with the controls and systems to focusing more on tactical decision-making. Experienced pilots eventually become one with the jet, their minds primarily centered on preemptive tactical strategy. I still had a long way to go.

The relentless engagement in afterburners rapidly depleted our fuel. I hit Joker Fuel and reset my bingo bug to bingo. We had just enough Jet A left for one more short round of fighting. At the start of our final round, we were over two nautical miles straight up, 12,500 feet above the ocean. I didn't consider the surface too much; I focused primarily on operating my radar with my new JHMCS helmet.

Spotting me in position abeam his jet, Diego called, "Speed and angels. Three, two, one, fight's on!" I engaged max afterburner and pulled the stick into my lap as we charged toward each other. As I started descending, the g-force tugged at my strained face. In the split second it took me to think about the HOTAS to operate my new helmet consciously, I slipped out of my habit of scanning my airspeed and altitude. Our paths crossed quickly at the merge. Already 30 degrees nose low and partially inverted, I rolled the jet fully inverted and dove downward in a split S maneuver.

As I descended rapidly toward the ocean, the jet accelerated. I raised my head against the strong g-force to keep sight of my adversary's aircraft above. Lose sight, lose the fight. The Super Hornet vibrated at seven and a half g's as the wings tore into the air, forcing the turn.

The bulky JHMCS helmet and my head usually weighed about twenty pounds at one g. Now, at approximately eight times the force of gravity, it felt like my head weighed nearly 160 pounds. I was pinned to the seat, struggling to breathe using the anti-G straining maneuver (AGSM). Unexpectedly, I felt the jet ease up at the worst possible moment. Without looking, I knew something was off. The g-force dropped from the expected seven and a half g's. Despite my control stick being pulled back into my lap, the jet was no longer obeying my commands. I was hurtling toward the ocean in a steep dive, out of control.

Time seemed to slow down. The pucker factor radically elevated. I pulled the throttles to idle and extended the speed brake desperately to regain control. In mere seconds, I'd gone from two miles above the ocean to an altitude where I could clearly see the foaming white caps and ripples on the turbulent waters below. The Ground Proximity Warning System detected the impending collision, triggering a blaring aural alert: "Pull up, pull up." The unresponsive stick was still pinned into my lap. My heart sank.

CHAPTER 2

I t's often said that when you have a near-death experience, your life flashes before your eyes. While my memories from this flirtation with death aren't entirely linear, there are glimpses of early experiences that took me from a mischievous, head-strong adolescent to a hopeful and equally stubborn young man determined to become an aviator.

I was born in Oklahoma in the mid-eighties, inheriting the stigma of being a so-called millennial snowflake from the get-go. My mother's medical school residency required much of her time and effort, making my father the primary caregiver for my younger sister and me.

By the time I was four, we lived in the rural Colorado town of Alamosa, nestled under the shadow of the southern Rocky Mountains. The clear blue skies usually lit up the contrasting arid landscape of the San Luis Valley. My mother had finished her residency and was fulfilling a scholarship program through the National Health Service. In exchange for a debt-free education, she worked in a rural area needing an obstetrician-gynecologist. Completing medical school at a time when being a female physician was still a controversial concept, her fierce determination to be respected as an equal fueled her passion for becoming a bona fide vagina whisperer.

I spent my early years chasing dust devils, discovering which colored ants would bite, and jumping my little red

Aspiring Ninja Turtle cowboy.

Gremlin bicycle over homemade ramps that progressively got larger with my friends. I wasn't allowed to have G.I. Joes or play violent video games, but when I hung out with my friends, I did all that and more. They had dirt bikes and a perilously balanced gas-powered three-wheeler that I loved to ride.

One neighborhood boy, eager to replicate stories of war, had dug intricate tunnels in his backyard. Despite my parents' warnings about the potential danger of cave-ins, I couldn't resist exploring the underground maze. One day, after navigating the dark passageways, I was invited into his home. The moment I stepped into the dimly lit double-wide trailer, I was hit with the pungent, stale odor of tobacco and cheap liquor that hung in the air like a fog.

The thick haze of cigarette smoke stung my eyes, making it hard to see at first. As my vision adjusted, I noticed the centerpiece of the room—a grizzled, obese man sitting in a worn-out recliner, an oxygen tube coiled around his face, connected to a green tank that hissed softly with each breath he took. This man was my friend's father, a Vietnam War veteran, now disabled and confined to a wheelchair. He was surrounded by a cluttered assortment of orange prescription bottles scattered across the side table, evidence of a lifetime's worth of pain and ailments.

His eyes were vacant, staring past the flickering television that played an endless stream of daytime talk shows. There was a heaviness in the air, a palpable sadness that seemed to seep from his very being. He didn't even flinch when we walked in, as though he had long grown numb to any sense of intrusion. It was as if he existed in a different world, one defined by the echoes of war and the constant hiss of his oxygen.

My friend moved about with familiarity, unfazed by the scene, but I felt an overwhelming sense of unease. This was my first encounter with the reality of what war could do to a person long after the fighting had ended. The sight of this man—broken, disconnected, and drowning in medication—left a mark on me, a haunting realization of how some battles never truly end. As we retreated back to the tunnels, I couldn't shake the image of him from my mind, a living reminder of the scars left behind by a conflict that had ended decades ago and another conflict that would afflict veterans for generations to come.

*   *   *

My uncle had served as a marine, but my father's number wasn't selected during the draft. Instead, he trained for Ironman Triathlons and mountain marathons, sometimes with me in tow.

He took me backcountry telemark skiing in a backpack and completed races while pushing me in a jogging stroller. I often wondered how my life would've turned out if our fathers' roles had been reversed. As it was, I considered myself fortunate.

Our family often drove up the frozen waterfall–lined highway to Wolf Creek Ski Area during winter weekends. The shimmering, light powder in the Southern Rockies was typically plentiful, usually well over my head. Within a year of learning to ski, I was hurtling down black diamond slopes with abandon. Weighing barely forty-something pounds, plunging into deep, fluffy powder meant wipeouts were harmless. I would pop up each time, dusted in a layer of glimmering white crystals, grinning widely and craving another run.

We moved to Northern Michigan around my seventh birthday. At that point, I was still unsure whether I wanted to be a cowboy, Ninja Turtle, or Ghostbuster. The mountain valleys gave way to woods, trickling streams, and freshwater lakes—my new playground. School was an unfortunate interruption to climbing trees, exploring, and playing soccer. My father, the mountain man, taught me to hunt, fish, backpack, and survive in the wilderness.

Dad trained for marathons and triathlons in old brown leather dress shoes. His missing toenails and cracked, bleeding heels made me question why anyone would pursue endurance sports. He frequently patched his worn clothes with mismatched materials, refusing to waste anything—including the frostbite-encased mystery foods at the bottom of our freezer. He could afford running shoes but was a die-hard conservationist. For fun, he swam year-round in Lake Michigan, carved his bows for hunting, and slept in snow caves. He was a wild man who didn't fit into modern society—this is a compliment, in my eyes. I was lucky to inherit his adventurous spirit.

For Halloween in second grade, Dad and I made a home-made rocket pack out of two-liter plastic bottles. We fashioned the iconic finned Rocketeer helmet from a plastic gallon milk jug and a strip of cardboard. A bit of bronze spray paint and duct tape later, I was ready to blast through the sky like Cliff Secord.

As a runty new kid with a rattail and a recycled garbage costume, I might as well have worn a sign that said, "Kick my ass." When the recess bell rang, a gang of older kids shoved me to the ground and smashed my rocket pack and helmet while I watched helplessly.

As I told my dad what happened, his brow furrowed. He taught me how to throw a punch and pointed out several vulnerable targets for self-defense. From then on, we often sparred. He was always encouraging but never let me win, emphasizing that these skills were for self-defense and protecting others.

Soon after the rocket pack incident, some older kids ganged up on me again. I was still an easy target, but they were in for a surprise this time. I unleashed a flurry of low punches, dropping one bully after another. Just as I started to feel invincible, they brushed themselves off, regrouped, and pushed me to the ground. They kicked me in the ribs as I curled up in a defensive fetal position. A mix of pride and burning rage welled up inside me.

Most of my free time was spent playing travel soccer. Despite my small stature, I was an agile and energetic defensive player. Often appointed team captain, I found myself learning leadership skills early on. Once, I stood up to a beast of a striker targeting me with underhanded shoves and kicks, rewarding his bullying with a surprise uppercut. With one swift strike, my fist connected with the giant's slack, mouth-breathing jaw, sending him into a state of unconsciousness. He crumpled to the ground, thumping against the earth like a fallen hardwood board.

The explosive cheer from my teammates and the subsequent confusion on the field was exhilarating. My father stood by my side when the other kid's dad confronted us. He replied matter-of-factly, "Your son started it. My son finished it."

Getting into fights landed me in the principal's office several times. (You could still have a scrap in the early nineties without getting expelled.) Growing tired of mindlessly filling out multiple-choice answers under the hum of fluorescent lights, I developed a skepticism toward authority. I knew I didn't want to live a life confined to filling boxes and earning gold stars. I wanted adventure.

A youth summer aviation course at Northwestern Michigan College was my gateway to the skies, an experience that transformed my youthful curiosity into a burning passion for flight. The classroom sessions were a whirlwind of new knowledge: weather patterns, aerodynamics, the intricate systems of aircraft, and the principles of flight operations. Each concept, meticulously explained by seasoned instructors, was a tiny glimpse into the vast world of aviation.

When the discovery flight was announced, anticipation crackled through me like electricity. A modest Cessna 152, little more than a winged lawnmower, awaited on the tarmac—a small craft that promised an immense adventure. Climbing into the cockpit, my hands were clammy with excitement, every nerve alive and alert. As I took hold of the yoke, the instructor's calm voice guided my actions, his presence a steadying force against my mounting exhilaration.

The engine roared to life, a mechanical heartbeat that quickened my own. With each instruction, I nudged the controls, the plane inching forward, gathering speed, until the runway was a blur beneath us. The ascent was gradual, the world tilting as we climbed higher. Despite its modest pace, in my heart, we might as well have been in a fighter jet blasting off with afterburners at full throttle.

Above, the landscape transformed. The vibrant turquoise hues of the Great Lakes stretched out beneath us, a sprawling canvas of water painted with strokes of brilliant azure and emerald. The ordinary world fell away, its troubles dwarfed by the vastness of the open sky. In that hour of flight, I was no longer bound by the limitations of the ground. I soared above it all, the freedom palpable, exhilarating.

More than the mechanics of flight captivated me—I loved the profound sense of liberation, the realization that the sky was not a limit but an invitation. As we descended back toward the runway, the experience settled deep within me. I knew then, with unwavering clarity, that my future was irrevocably linked to the boundless skies. This flight wasn't just an introduction but also the beginning of a lifelong journey—a commitment to chasing the freedom that only the heavens could offer.

CHAPTER 3

My mom was often called into surgery at odd hours. Dad did his best to cover. Both my parents prioritized savings for travel over buying shiny, new possessions. As a result, I had the privilege of seeing many national parks on our family road trips. We almost always camped in tents. I vividly recall clambering over massive rock arches, the sulfuric smell of geysers, picking M&Ms out of my trail mix during navigational blunders, and nearly toppling over the edge of the Grand Canyon. Those experiences, rich with adventure and awe, shaped my character and cemented my love for the great outdoors.

Trips out west with my mother to medical conferences were filled with contradictions. On the surface, they were a young boy's adventure through swag bags stuffed with pharmaceutical logos and mysterious adult exchanges that floated over my head. Yet these excursions were also a rare window into the life of my mother, a driven, independent woman enmeshed deeply in the dance between medicine and the pharmaceutical industry.

While she absorbed the latest drug advancements, her dedication was palpable. She wasn't just attending these conferences to get in some skiing; she was also fighting to stay ahead in a profession that demanded her all. Her tenacity and hard work had allowed her to persevere in an industry then dominated by men. And in those moments, as I watched her navigate through dense medical jargon and industry politics,

I noticed her resilience and dedication. She was scrappy, yet I could see the toll it took on her. She was divided between her drive to succeed as a physician and her role as a mother. Her frequent absences took a toll on our bond, but at least we got a little time to enjoy the mountains together.

As my mother delved into the world of pharmaceutical presentations, I escaped to the slopes. The Rockies became my refuge, with their steep double black diamonds and treacherous moguls. During one particularly windy ride on a narrow two-person chairlift, I nearly fell, my tree-climbing instincts kicking in just in time to save me. Such moments of peril strangely paralleled my mother's precarious balance in her professional life, always on the brink yet somehow managing to hold on.

CHAPTER 4

In high school, I was a bit of an academic slacker—dozing off in class or skipping it entirely. Still, I managed decent grades with minimum effort by mastering the art of multiple-choice tests. I dismissed most homework as an unwelcome intrusion into my free time.

For a video production class, my friends and I filmed a *Jackass*-style stunt movie. My classmates received it with delight until the scene with a homemade flamethrower—a contraption I had created using a modified Super Soaker filled with a mixture of gasoline and Styrofoam. The erupting flames were enough to halt the premiere and earn us a visit to the principal's office, resulting in a three-day suspension. On reflection, we were lucky the device hadn't exploded.

The fallout included a lesson from my mom, who brought home medical textbooks featuring burn victims and severe venereal diseases. While it was a sobering reality check, the graphic content did help prevent any early fatherhood aspirations and curb my pyromaniac tendencies.

Learning to drive my dad's poop brown 1985 Honda Civic was an escapade. It was an old, manual vehicle with crank windows and a floor riddled with holes. After mastering the gears and clutch, I gained the privilege of driving my mom's Subaru. The all-wheel drive, coupled with an abundance of dirt roads in our area, resulted in some overconfidence and a newfound hobby of drift driving.

To curb my reckless driving, my parents enrolled me in a defensive driving course offered by the local police department. The course, which took place in an iced-over section of the local airport, aimed to teach students how to handle sudden and unexpected situations. However, given my extensive experience drifting on icy roads and doing donuts in parking lots, I found the course comically easy. I took particular delight in the instructors' visible frustration as they failed to make me lose control of the vehicle, even with abrupt pulls of the emergency brake.

However, this didn't stop my speeding, and the following year, I accumulated a fair share of tickets while blasting gangster rap, behaving like some witless fusion of Jesse Pinkman and Napoleon Dynamite. One night, while speeding down an unfamiliar dirt road, I crashed the car, bouncing off trees like a pinball before coming to a stop. The car was wrecked, but the airbags prevented injury. Something was gnawing at me from the inside, driving me to reckless behavior. Some deep-seated anger was simmering within my core. The more I tried to bottle it back up, the more it seemed to overflow.

I grappled with the weight of situational depression during my teenage years. Eventually, I was diagnosed with seasonal affective disorder. The culprit was supposedly the lack of sunshine during the gray winter months in Northern Michigan, though I now suspect there was far more to it.

My psychiatrist, a stout man with the demeanor and appearance of a confused walrus, prescribed me Luvox, an SSRI antidepressant, as a remedy. Dutifully, I took the medication for months, waiting for some shift in my mood, a spark of normalcy that never came. With each passing day, the pill felt more like a placebo, offering no tangible relief from the growing storm inside me.

My parents, desperate for answers, placed their hopes on the medication. They were eager for me to fit in at school, to calm the growing rage that was becoming harder to hide. Their belief in conventional medicine was unwavering. If the doctors said a pill could help, then surely it would. But as the months passed with no improvement, they seemed resigned, as if they, too, were slowly detaching from the reality that their son was still struggling. My mother, consumed by her overwhelming career, was forced to outsource her care to specialists. My father put his faith in the medical professionals and followed my mom's guidance.

Without a word to them, I made my decision. The Luvox pills, which were supposed to fix me, began to pile up in secret. I couldn't bear to continue taking something that felt so meaningless. I hid them away, stashing them in places where no one would find them, all the while trying to mask the inner chaos.

Looking back now, I realize how often these medications are handed to teenagers like me as the first, and sometimes only, line of defense. There's an unsettling truth in the way depression is treated—SSRIs are prescribed without much consideration of alternative therapies or long-term effects. Recent research even suggests that much of the so-called "scientific basis" for these treatments has been shaped and driven by the pharmaceutical industry's vested interest in profit over genuine patient care.

It's a sobering realization. The widespread reliance on medication, often marketed as a cure-all for mental health, rests on a fragile foundation—especially for vulnerable young people. This quick-fix approach makes me wonder if it's doing more harm than good. Shouldn't we be looking for a more holistic, patient-centered path to healing? Perhaps the issue lies not with the children but with the unnatural environments we force them into—disrupted sleep, harsh, fluorescent lights, hours indoors filling out worksheets, and ultra-processed cafeteria food. The further we distance ourselves from nature, the sicker we become.

I discovered an unconventional solution to my depression accidentally when I ingested a handful of crunchy little mushrooms during a campfire gathering with a small group of close friends. The effects were startlingly profound. I was mesmerized by the dynamic embers of the fire. After hours of watching the glowing coals in awe, I ventured inside and looked at my reflection. I hallucinated black, snakelike threads seeping from the pores on my face. While initially terrified, I reminded myself that it was a hallucination. When I closed my eyes as the experience intensified, I was awash in a shimmering network of interconnected stars and threads, an overwhelmingly beautiful representation of the universe. The experience was life-changing and reconnected me to the universe in a way I hadn't felt before.

Waking up the morning after, I found the world transformed. I reveled in the simple pleasures of sunlight and the scent of the forest, taking joy in the vibrancy of the leaves. With my depression seemingly vanishing, I felt a newfound connection to everything around me.

This renewed zest for life led to an increased engagement at school. I became more involved in extracurricular activities, serving as a soccer and wrestling team captain. Wrestling season was particularly grueling, often involving lunch breaks spent running laps around the gym in a sweat suit to cut weight while dreaming of cold sports drinks and cheeseburgers. While I still had little patience for mundane busy work, I demonstrated commitment and discipline toward what I deemed essential.

High school graduation was a liberating moment for me. Barefoot and elated, I was glad to be free from the routine monotony of school and eager to embark on the next chapter of my life. My parents, too, were relieved and happy to see me graduate without having to bail me out of jail. Little did they know the many adventures awaiting me in the coming years.

CHAPTER 5

The aviation program at Northwestern Michigan College from years prior had left a lasting impression on me, namely my discovery of flight. My first job had been washing dishes and bussing tables at a perpetually understaffed diner, earning a paltry five dollars an hour. Amid the pungent smell of the grease trap and a coworker's strange fascination with killing trapped flies by blowing smoke into a pint glass prison, I realized I wanted more from life.

I also knew a lifetime spent boxed in an office cubicle wasn't for me. Aviation struck me as the ideal blend of a respectable career and a continuous adventure. My long-term aspiration was to establish a floatplane company, guiding passengers to secluded destinations for surfing, kiteboarding, fishing, and hunting to escape conventional societal structures—to be free.

A handful of friends I made during my first semester of college asked me to move into an old beach house on Lake Michigan with them. The house was due to be leveled to make way for a grand mansion, and the owner seemed content to rent it out to a lively bunch of college lads—we could initiate the demolition work for him. While I partook in the occasional rowdy house parties, I was adamant about putting my studies first to swiftly secure my private pilot certificate, instrument rating, and commercial certification.

Our house parties had a reputation for being fun, and before long, they started attracting some beautiful women from the local college. One regular was a sharp, petite blonde named Cara with an adventurous spirit that immediately stood out. Word around the house was that she grew up sailing the Caribbean with her family—a modern-day hippie pirate. Though we didn't interact much then, fate had bigger plans. Little did I know, our paths would cross again a decade later.

The summer following my freshman year brought a new adventure. My childhood buddy Max had won free kiteboarding lessons from Broneah Kiteboarding and asked me to accompany him. We devoted two days to learning the basics of handling the powerful kites without putting ourselves in mortal danger. The thrill of gliding over water and launching high into the sky was unlike any other sport I had experienced. Post-tutorial, I approached the young owners of the Broneah Kiteboarding shop, Matt and Keegan Myers, inquiring about any budget-friendly used kites they might have. They unearthed an old Naish X2 C kite with bare-minimum safety features and no depower. For a mere three hundred dollars, I walked out of the shop, my very first kite, bar, lines, and used harness in tow. A board was beyond my financial reach, but at least I could start mastering the kite.

Like a true enthusiast, I monitored the wind forecast relentlessly. Any hint of winds surpassing ten knots would find me on the beach, wrestling with the gusts before heading to work, content and sun-kissed. My evenings were spent waiting tables at an Italian-style wine bar, serving spirits to disgruntled tourists who had just endured a full day's drive to escape suburbia in minivans packed with their rowdy offspring.

While learning to kiteboard, I had several brushes with danger. The long kite lines often ensnared me, pulling me under the water, out of control. As the lines dragged me face-first through Lake Michigan, they lacerated my skin. I had to stay composed, disentangle myself, and regain control of the kite to avoid drowning or colliding with a dock. Little did I know that this ordeal would serve as valuable training in the future.

Young me enjoying some kiteboarding on Lake Michigan during college, featuring a fresh black eye courtesy of a surfboard to the face a few days prior.

Matt and Keegan from Broneah Kiteboarding often noticed my blue kite as they ferried students to their secret lesson spot. The following summer, I approached Broneah, enquiring about instructor vacancies. They welcomed me onto their team. On my first day of lessons, I arrived wearing an outdated shirt I'd found at a thrift shop. Matt and Keegan winced as they handed me a brand-new Broneah T-shirt.

"Stick to wearing this," Matt gently advised.

CHAPTER 6

The Michigan summers were idyllic by the Great Lakes, but the winters came with the advantage of relative solitude. On a particularly harsh late-winter day, my housemates and I were transfixed by the sight of towering waves cresting, curling, and breaking at a sandbar some quarter mile offshore. A gusty northern storm was blowing snow sideways in the blizzard, conjuring up a formidable swell that could have been the centerpiece of a freshwater surf documentary. Scott, one of my housemates, had an open-hull aluminum fishing boat stored on our beach, a relic from his grandfather. As we gazed at the impressive waves breaking and rolling toward the ice-encrusted shore, one of us spoke to the daredevil plan we'd all been silently contemplating: Why not take the fishing boat out and surf those waves? What could possibly go wrong?

Donning a wet suit more suited for mild summer days than near-freezing water temperatures, I layered up with my winter shell jacket and snow pants—not exactly the right gear for these conditions. Still, it was what I had on hand. We geared up as best we could and headed to the snow-blasted beach.

Our first few attempts went surprisingly well. We motored past the Deepwater Point sandbar, about a quarter mile offshore where the lake bed dropped off. This area had been used for logging, creating a natural, log-laden, reef-like structure, now blanketed in sand. It was an excellent spot for a good break when strong northern winds whipped through. The winds were howling, and the choppy waves churned. The spitting water's icy sting on our exposed faces was hair-raising. Scott skillfully steered us into the break, then lined us up with an incoming swell. With the precise turn and rev of the engine, we rode the jagged surf, the thrill making my heart pound as a head-high wave crashed just behind us.

Elated by our initial success, I briefly shrugged off the cold. We veered toward the break for another set. As the snow fell on our wind-chapped faces, a sizeable swell loomed ahead. Scott revved the engine and steered us into it, but a rogue wave blind-sided us. Our intrepid dingy rapidly capsized.

Thrown into the frigid waves a quarter mile from the shore, I gasped as I surfaced, the icy water burning against my skin. My snow pants and jacket had filled with water, making swimming hard. I kicked off my waterlogged boots but kept my wet gloves on for some semblance of warmth. As I took stock of the situation and began to swim toward the shore, Scott helped our other housemate, Joe, who was already struggling from the onset of hypothermia in his shorty wet suit. Despite my full-length wet suit, I could feel my limbs quickly losing function, but I was determined to reach the shore.

When we returned to shore, my extremities were numb and barely responding. A neighbor rushed toward us, informing us that the Coast Guard was about to dispatch a helicopter. Back at the house, my hands were so numb that I struggled to peel off my soaked gear. Various first responder vehicles filled our driveway, and the Coast Guard helicopter call-off arrived just in time to avoid a five-thousand-dollar bill. The grin on one of the volunteer firefighters told me he understood our reckless urge. I would rather risk death for a taste of adventure than merely exist without truly living.

The shower I took that day was almost as memorable as the misadventure. Even the initial cold water felt soothingly warm compared to the raging freshwater ocean I had just emerged from. Our escapade made headlines in the local *Record-Eagle* newspaper.

CHAPTER 7

I was a certified flight instructor during my senior year at Northwestern Michigan College. Because I was the smallest flight instructor, I was granted an unexpected distinction: I became the aerobatics instructor. Northwestern Michigan College boasted a modest Cessna 152 Aerobat, a tiny craft with limited payload capacity, capable of accommodating only two souls. With my trim physique, barely tipping the scales at 130 pounds even in my wettest state, ample room remained for a normal-sized human to join me in the cramped cockpit. My mission became to teach others the art of aerial acrobatics, unveiling the secrets of looping, barrel rolling, snap rolling, and spinning. In those exhilarating moments amidst the heavens, the boundaries of gravity dissolved, and my students and I reveled in the sublime liberation of flight.

As an instructor, I was tasked with mentoring a middle-aged gentleman named Larry, who was starting his aviation journey. Before I met him, tales of his intriguing persona floated around our workspaces, painting him as a mysterious character right out of a James Bond movie. The idea of working with him excited me.

Larry had served in the US Navy as a forensic accountant during the Vietnam War. When US forces discovered document troves in the hidden tunnels of the Viet Cong, Special Forces would escort Larry in to investigate. Blessed with a photographic memory, a knack for languages, and a sharp intellect, he was adept at reviewing financial data to uncover the origin of weapon funding, subsequently debriefing US intelligence. During one such mission, he took a powerful round of 7.62mm in the back but recovered from the devastating bullet wound.

After his prestigious military career, Larry amassed an impressive array of doctorate degrees from reputed institutions, including Carnegie Mellon. He earned a presidential award for his academic excellence, with a cumulative GPA over 4.0. He laid the groundwork for a think tank. Larry carved a niche as a privacy consultant, guiding many renowned firms in shaping their privacy norms.

During our inaugural lesson, I assigned Larry an aircraft systems test to complete. He presented the completed paper in the following session, his handwriting so precise that it seemed almost robotic. Each system was meticulously drawn. By the end of a semester's worth of lessons, he extended a job offer to me. He planned on purchasing an aircraft for his firm and wished me to pilot it. Given the turbulence in the airline industry back then, securing a job that provided a decent wage was a challenge for many instructors. I was extraordinarily fortunate to receive such an opportunity.

Larry's company acquired a brand-new Mooney Acclaim, an aircraft modeled after the iconic WWII fighter, the P-51 Mustang. It was the epitome of luxury in general aviation, equipped with hand-stitched leather seats and state-of-the-art glass panel avionics, complete with an integrated autopilot. The aircraft's powerful engine marked a significant upgrade from the Cessna models that were my usual teaching tools. I spent the year crisscrossing the United States after training at the Mooney factory in Texas. Sometimes, I would instruct Larry on these trips. However, much of the flying was solo, offering ample room to exercise my decision-making skills and learn from my errors.

During a summer afternoon flight from a southern expedition, we contended with an advancing line of insidious embedded thunderstorms. Using radar images beamed to our screens from satellites, we plotted a course through the maelstrom—or so we thought. We thought we would clear an upcoming cell well before its arrival. Still, lagging radar refresh rates gave us a false sense of security. Being engulfed in the clouds made it impossible to see where the towering cells were visually.

From the seemingly safe inside of a bright, white cloud, we plunged into tempestuous, dark purple chaos without warning. Fat drops of rain pelted against the windscreen as our aircraft underwent severe turbulence. We lurched between being pinned to our seats and dangling from our seatbelts while being flung about by the tempest's powerful, shearing updrafts and downdrafts. We were as helpless as a squeaky toy in the mouth of an enraged pit bull. Lightning danced around us, painting the cabin with brief, terrifying illuminations. Our arms flailed as we struggled to maintain control. As abruptly as it had begun, the storm relinquished us, and we emerged miraculously unscathed on the other side. Almost in mockery, the weather radar updated the moment we regained control to show we had just survived flying through the heart of an embedded thunderstorm.

Larry and I began test-flying more capable business aircraft like the Citation Mustang and TBM 850, hopeful to upgrade the company from the piston-powered Mooney Acclaim. Given the frequent long-distance travel in adverse weather, the latter needed more capabilities for frequent West Coast trips. Many of these trips culminated in evenings of fine dining and exquisite wine, which, while plush, eventually became routine.

When the stock market crashed, the aspirations of an aircraft upgrade evaporated like the middle class. I considered pursuing medical school and started volunteering in an emergency room. It did not take long to realize I lacked empathy for caring for the morbidly obese, alcoholic individuals who patronized the hospital. I began toying with the idea of buying a van and setting off on a nomadic adventure with my kiteboarding gear, mountain bike, and backpacking equipment. Had I done so, I would have had very different experiences to write about.

*   *   *

A fellow flight instructor from Northwestern Michigan College, Mark Hall, was preparing his application for the US Navy's Officer Candidate School (OCS) to secure a pilot slot. Up until then, I was under the impression that only those who attended the Naval Academy and had admirals for fathers could fly for the navy. It seemed improbable for a community college kid like me to fly fighter jets like Maverick.

One of my college professors, Commander Mike Stock (Ret.), is a legendary naval aviator with a storied career. Initially serving as a Huey gunship helicopter pilot during the Vietnam War, he flew high-risk missions for the first special operations helicopter units, the Seawolves. These volunteer pilots were tasked with flying operators into the heart of danger, in any weather and at any hour. Uniforms were unnecessary, as were formal titles. Everyone was there because of their passion and willingness to risk their lives for their compatriots. Amidst the most perilous of flying conditions, he survived.

Later in his career, he became a test pilot, flying a myriad of aircraft, from fighter jets to the colossal Piasecki PA-97 Helistat. This behemoth of an aircraft was a heavy-lift helium airship equipped with four mounted helicopters constructed to aid the National Forest Service in logging remote locations. It stands as the largest aircraft ever built. To provide a sense of scale, if an NFL stadium were devoid of goalposts, the Helistat would barely fit within.

Despite hearing trepidation from an experienced engineer friend, Mr. Stock was seduced by the opportunity to make the first flight on such a historic aircraft. Initial hover tests were successful, but tragedy struck during flight testing. The absence of vibration-reducing shimmy dampeners on the wheels made the aluminum frame collapse during its inaugural forward flight, just a few miles from where the Hindenburg exploded. This collapse was reminiscent of an overloaded shopping cart— when pushed too fast, the wheels shake so violently that the entire cart collapses. Remarkably, he survived the crash without major physical injuries.

Mr. Stock has documented his incredible flying career in several books, including *Chasing the Four Winds*. The Helistat crash was also featured in a History Channel documentary. After yet another risky life chapter as an Alaskan bush pilot, he earned the FAA's esteemed Master Pilot Award. In his forty-year career, he defied the odds to miraculously survive seven crashes in his pursuit of adventure.

Having him as an instructor and mentor was a privilege. His tales of adventure kindled an attraction to military flying within me. However, Mr. Stock never explicitly encouraged us to pursue this path. He, more than most, knew it was a perilous aspiration. When Mark shared his ambitions, I realized it could be a viable option for me.

Determined to learn everything possible about a career in military aviation, I voraciously devoured information from an online forum called Airwarriors.com. The forum, operated by military pilots, provides invaluable resources and insights into pursuing this career path. After a thorough investigation, I confirmed I had a solid chance for a pilot slot and applied to US Navy OCS. Weeks later, I got word from my recruiter: I was accepted to OCS. The stoke of my acceptance and the support of friends and family drove me as I readied my mind and body for the challenge awaiting me.

One of the most crucial aspects of preparing for OCS is physical conditioning. While it's not necessary to be an elite athlete, it's vital to be comfortable moving your body weight. A regimen of calisthenics (such as push-ups, sit-ups, and air squats) combined with running is an excellent starting point. In preparation, I started training at a CrossFit gym called Leading Edge Fitness, managed by a marine, Billy G. I was about to spend thirteen weeks under strenuous marine drill instructor training, so it made sense to have a head start.

My first workout consisted of several hundred yards of lunges for a warm-up, followed by "Fran," a notoriously grueling CrossFit workout. "Fran" includes barbell thrusters and pull-ups, alternating between twenty-one-, fifteen-, and nine-repetition sets. The combination of these exercises quickly drove my heart rate through the roof, leaving my arms and legs trembling. Even with a barbell loaded thirty pounds lighter than the standard weight for men, I could barely lift my arms by the end of the workout, and my legs were so weak that I crumbled to the ground. Gasping for air, I didn't know if I would vomit, cry, lose bowel control, or combine all three. I spent a solid week limping around as I recovered.

Once capable of squatting onto a toilet again, I returned for more. Seeing my return, Billy G smiled and quipped, "I didn't think we would ever see you again." In just a couple of months,

I gained twenty pounds of lean muscle, making me faster and stronger than ever before.

I participated in the inaugural M22 Challenge, a triathlon created by my friends at Broneah and their emerging M22 company. M22 is an iconic road that graces the northwestern coast of Michigan's lower peninsula, with its picturesque rolling green hills and mesmerizingly clear blue water—truly a perfect venue for a triathlon. I finished sixth overall, just behind an Olympian, and managed to outrank a recon marine and several collegiate and professional athletes. I was glowing and in peak physical and mental condition. I was ready for OCS.

As I was about to depart, Mr. Stock presented me with a bottle. He told me there would come a day in my military career when I'd feel an overpowering desire to give up. When that day arrived, he suggested I open the bottle and enjoy a libation to rejuvenate my spirit. I held the hope that such a day would never come. Then, in the autumn of 2009, with my car packed with only a few personal belongings, I embarked on a journey to Newport, Rhode Island, eager and prepared to turn over a new leaf in my life.

CHAPTER 8

Crossing the suspension bridge leading to Naval Station Newport, I was brimming with anticipation to begin Officer Candidate School. I felt prepared, though I had no illusion that I was headed for a leisurely vacation. I envisioned OCS as a boot camp for prospective officers, expecting endless yelling, running, and countless push-ups. Scenes from the movie *Full Metal Jacket* were firmly lodged in my mind. I was aware that the marine drill instructors would push us nasty navy officer candidates to our limits, and oddly, I found myself looking forward to the challenge. After all, I'd mentally and physically exerted myself far worse than any drill instructor could.

Upon arrival, we were checked in by officer candidates clad in their new khaki uniforms. They were in their final weeks of training. Despite having been in our boots just months before, some of the upperclassmen exuded an air of superiority that bordered on hilarity. As we unloaded in front of the aged building that would be our home for the next three months, an eerie silence hung in the air. We all knew things were about to get intense.

The moment the door closed behind us, a cacophony of shouting filled the stairwell. Upperclassmen hurled orders, herding us haphazardly toward our rooms. Many candidates were visibly scared, overwhelmed by the unfolding chaos.

I, however, was strangely calm, even enjoying the mayhem around me. This was precisely the experience I'd prepared for.

We had a few indoctrination candidates drop-on-request (DOR) from day one. In other words, they quit just because they had to shave their heads. I couldn't fathom what they thought they were signing up for. Some candidates couldn't complete a mile-and-a-half run to save their lives. Another candidate was so unfit that they didn't survive the first morning standing at attention. Indoctrination candidates dropping like flies so early in training was concerning, but my preparation fueled my confidence.

Every morning began at a chilly zero dark thirty, well before dawn. The drill instructors unleashed a symphony of tirades, melding physical training (PT) with relentless vocal assaults. At the physical training sessions, I was perpetually amazed by the number of candidates who came to OCS without adequate preparation, their bodies not conditioned for the demands ahead. Yet some among us were primed, ready to conquer.

After we had a chance to settle into our pleasant accommodations, we were herded into a queue for a battery of vaccinations. Despite having brought my updated vaccination records, I suspect they were promptly filed in the shredder, as I was given what felt like every vaccine ever created, all at once. From being at the pinnacle of my fitness, I plummeted into a lingering illness that persisted for months. I was plagued with a constant, green discharge from my nose, and my body alternated between fever and chills. I was significantly weaker than usual, and concentrating was a struggle. Like many others, I sucked it up and soldiered on.

Soon after being vaccinated, we had our first room inspection. We spent days preparing all our gear. Everything had to be folded precisely, and a plethora of knowledge had to be committed to memory. It demanded acute attention to detail. Confident that everything was in order, I stood at attention in front of my room as the inspectors arrived.

A doughy navy lieutenant approached me, and I snapped off a textbook-perfect salute. He deducted points for every aspect of my salute, justified or not. As he entered my room ahead of me, I watched him covertly pull a pair of balled-up, dirty socks from his pocket and toss them onto my dresser. Feigning surprise, he acted as though I had carelessly left them there. He then tore apart every piece of my meticulously folded clothing, penalizing me for virtually everything. I realized this was a test; unable to break me with PT, they wanted to see how I'd handle unjust failure. So I stood there silently, bearing it all as I continued to stand at attention—an invaluable skill to acquire in the military.

After thirteen weeks of PT, rifle drill, academics, memorizing endless, pointless facts, and restraining laughter at the constant absurdity, I graduated from OCS. I donned the rank of the mighty ensign, O-1, or as it's commonly called, "butter bar." It signifies to the enlisted ranks that we outrank them but have no idea what the hell we're doing. My family attended the formal graduation ceremony. I was proud of my accomplishment, but my nerves were anxious, anticipating what was to come. I was relieved to eat with a fork again as I drove to sunny Pensacola, Florida, to start flight school.

Unfortunately, due to widespread military budget cuts, the navy found they had too many student naval aviators (SNAs) for their allocated funding. To rectify the surplus, the leadership began deploying various creative strategies to trim our numbers.

The entire aviation pathway was congested with a shortage of funds and a grounded fleet of training aircraft, creating a bottleneck in the pipeline. In contrast, the fleet suffered a worsening pilot deficiency. What was supposed to be a six-week-long course took over six months just to get started for many SNAs. Armed with disposable income and minimal responsibilities, most took this opportunity to partake in copious amounts of merrymaking. Those impounded at the Naval Academy throughout their precious university years commonly overcompensated for their lack of a genuine college experience.

To address the overpopulation, students were initially offered the option to be redesignated into other navy communities, such as intelligence, JAG, and supply. Students already jaded after four years of sanctioned naval hazing at the Academy or ROTC were permitted to vacate the military with a free, four-year degree.

However, when these initial efforts failed to reduce the hordes of underutilized and party-happy butter bars sufficiently, the passing grade was raised from the easily achievable 80 percent minimum of yesteryears to the mid-nineties. This meant we had to score an A on every exam, or our dreams would be shattered. Historically, aviation preflight indoctrination (API) was a relaxed training evolution. However, the atmosphere quickly turned tense as students began failing in droves.

Shortly after I started API, the pressure to reduce numbers grew desperate. Leadership implemented Project Nightmare Oprah. One morning at muster, the hungover SNAs waiting to start were asked to check under their randomly assigned seats. Anyone who found a pink envelope was cut from the training. Morale took a nosedive.

After starting the course, the rotund instructor grimly warned us to look around the room in one of our first lessons. He soberly noted that some of us would likely perish in this career. Like most other students, I naively assumed that would never happen to me. I convinced myself I would study hard enough and be proficient enough to avoid that outcome.

The minimum test score required to pass continued to rise. After each exam, grades were posted on a wall in the main hallway. We would all flock to see our fate. Many people didn't make it. Only about half of my API class graduated from the academic portion to start aviation survival training.

Aviation survival training included a mile-long swim in a baggy flight suit and steel-toe boots. Several more students dropped out. Next was underwater egress training in the helo dunker. The helo dunker is a helicopter fuselage that flips occupants upside down in a pool to simulate a helicopter crash.

Due to the weight of the roof-mounted engines, helicopter crashes into the ocean often flip upside-down, frequently drowning occupants as they struggle to escape. In the dunker, students must remain calm and hold their breath, disconnect their harnesses, and swim through a hatch to reach the surface for air. Once students complete a few rides with their vision intact, they must escape blindfolded. This would be chaotic and terrifying in real life, especially in the dark, murky ocean, but it was enjoyable in the heated, calm pool (at least for some of us). Due to the recent Deepwater Horizon oil spill in the Gulf, several of our ocean survival exercises were canceled. A few were completed in a heated pool. Hopefully, we would never need those skills.

After completing API, I found myself in a holding pattern called C-pool as I awaited my orders for primary flight training. With time on my hands and a steady income, I embraced the laid-back atmosphere of Pensacola, partaking in a range of shenanigans that quickly ate into my earnings.

I recall one such evening at the historical Pensacola Officers Club, where I found myself in a dice game with a grizzled pilot from the Vietnam era. We had a riotous time that evening as we butter bars, outfitted in our newly issued, crispy flight suits, continually supplied the spirited, retired veteran with drinks. But also, we young, aspiring aviators gathered around our festive table gleaned more about naval aviation from this salty old air warrior than we had from all our formal training up to that point.

CHAPTER 9

After some more "hurry up and wait" in Pensacola, my orders finally came through. I was assigned to VT-28 Rangers in Corpus Christi, Texas. There I'd be flying the T-34C Turbo Mentor, a high-performance, fully aerobatic turboprop aircraft, which was a significant upgrade from the small Cessnas I used to instruct in. With a few friends from OCS, we managed to score a condo on North Padre Island a block from the beach. I was thrilled to be back in the cockpit.

The commanding officer, a burly, former H-60 Seahawk helicopter pilot, conducted our introductory briefing. When he asked us what we wanted to fly, most students gave the well-rehearsed reply, "Sir, I would just be happy to have the opportunity to fly anything, sir." I, however, committed the faux pas of being honest and expressed my desire to fly F/A-18s.

Primary flight training was conducted mainly by P-3 Orion patrol pilots and H-60 helicopter pilots. Some of them harbor lingering bitterness from not getting their chance at jets, so hearing a fresh-faced student boldly proclaiming ambitions of becoming a fighter pilot rubbed some of them the wrong way. I could almost feel their penetrating glares.

Despite my readiness, the ongoing backlog in the flight training pipeline delayed my first flight. So, I put my downtime to good use and dove deep into my studies. Over a few weeks, I memorized all the emergency procedures, standard operating procedures, course rules, and aircraft systems. Being proactive in naval flight training paid off, and it was soon that my preparation and discipline would reap their rewards.

I reported for my first lesson well prepared. My strict instructor, a former E-2 Hawkeye pilot, seemed only slightly less irritated when I quickly answered the planned lesson topics. Despite his skepticism, he was satisfied with my knowledge level for the day, and we geared up to head to the flight line.

Suppose you wish to have someone sit directly behind you, continuously berating you as you attempt to operate an unfamiliar aircraft while sweating profusely in the Texas sun. In that case, naval flight training is for you. Despite the constant verbal onslaught and high expectations, the flights could be enjoyable, at least once in a while. Despite the seemingly objective grading standards, it was clear that personalities influenced the final grades nearly as much as performance.

The simulators were condoned torture. The antiquated T-34 simulators were the size of a coffin, seated on a mechanical bull–like device designed to induce motion sickness. You were left to navigate solely by the disorganized steam gauge instruments. The grumpy old simulator instructors did their best to make our lives miserable while regaling us with stories of their glory days like Uncle Rico.

The simulator was a testing ground for complex emergency procedures, requiring blind manipulation of dozens of switches and circuit breakers while flying in bad weather, executing unexpected reroutes, and managing a range of other absurd scenarios. It wasn't just about honing our flying skills but also about assessing how we'd handle stress. We joked that the prehistoric simulator instructors plugged their headsets into the consoles to drain us of our youth and vitality, rejuvenating themselves for their next round of golf.

The following eight months were spent learning system knowledge, basic flight operations, instrument flying, aerobatics, and formation flying. The navy has a remarkable knack for compressing an enormous amount of training into a brief syllabus. Despite the instructors' relentless efforts to make flying a grueling endeavor, there were moments when I found it genuinely enjoyable. However, the continuous grading somewhat took the edge off the thrill. I began to acclimate to the constant pressure of having my career hanging in the balance. On any given day, a mistake could derail our dreams.

When not studying, I spent my free time hitting the gym with a solid group of aspiring aviators. We had a friendly rivalry going, spurring each other on to get faster and stronger through our grueling overkill versions of the CrossFit workout of the day. The weekends offered a chance to let off steam, with barhopping at The Pelican on North Padre Island a popular choice. The consistent trade winds on Padre Island made for some excellent kiteboarding. However, the glassy inland water fumed a subtle aroma of raw sewage.

During primary training, a fellow student and instructor were forced to bail out when their T-34C spiraled into an inverted spin. With no ejection seat in the T-34C, they manually opened the canopy, disconnected their harnesses, and jumped out while tumbling toward the earth. They were both fortunate to escape unharmed. The Turbo Mentor wreckage made for a nice fishing reef. In part, I was envious that the student got to skydive from an out-of-control aircraft.

I managed to graduate second in my class and was thrilled to select the tailhook pipeline on my dream sheet. To make the cut for tailhook, you had to score in the top 50 percent of what was known as the Navy Standard Score (NSS). Helicopters, P-3 patrol planes, and E-9s were also potential options for student aviators. Still, sometimes, the needs of the navy meant that even those with jet-worthy grades didn't get their first choice. I was lucky to secure a slot for T-45C Goshawk train-ing in Kingsville, Texas, and was off to fly jets. Completing the strenuous eight-month primary flight training syllabus made me one step closer to my dream job and provided a breath of relief. That night, we damn near burned down The Pelican as we celebrated like rock stars.

CHAPTER 10

My intermediate flight training in the T-45C Goshawk had been relatively smooth. My outstanding grades placed me at the top of my class, and there were only a few flights left before I had to face another selection round. The remaining flights were an introduction to tactical formation, or tac-form, which involved maneuvering the jet at a mile or more distances to stay in the correct position relative to the flight lead. It was an essential foundational skill for eventually flying tactical aircraft—if I made it that far. I'd mastered close formation flying, so tac-form seemed straightforward enough in theory. That overconfidence led me into the flight with a carefree attitude.

For the first time in my naval flight training, I began to struggle. The geometry of maneuvering at these extended ranges was trickier than I anticipated. My instructor, Vern, growing increasingly frustrated with my performance, only heightened my distress. By the time we landed, I knew I had to re-fly the event. I had earned a dreaded pink sheet, a failing grade, now permanently recorded in my flight training jacket as a signal of difficulty (SOD).

Determined to overcome this setback, I spent the following day studying tac-form techniques and geometry. Despite my newfound understanding, the fear of failing this re-fly was overpowering. Vern, with whom I had a good rapport outside the cockpit, was once again tasked with supervising my flight.

Unfortunately, my performance mirrored my previous attempt. I simply couldn't maintain a proper position. The twin burden of failing before a mentor and the fear of a career-ending pink slip loomed large. My previous flight experience, which had mostly been a boon so far, was no help in this new challenge. It was a harsh reality check.

The next day, I had to take the infamous "walk of shame" into the squadron, dressed in my khaki uniform instead of my flight suit—a sign to everyone that I'd fucked up. I had to face my class advisor, a former C-2 COD pilot named Drifter, who was known for his refreshingly relaxed personality. Legendary tales surrounded him, from making boot soles out of beef jerky before SERE school to breaking out of his cell and freeing his classmates. His brilliant antics had reportedly led to a revamp of the rules at SERE school. Rumor has it that Drifter retired on the per diem money he'd saved while flying CODs and now lives off the grid on a sailboat, flying gliders. If the world ever ends, you'll find Drifter on his sailboat with a beautiful woman enjoying the rock of the ocean.

Drifter spoke to me candidly. My rapid fall from grace, from the top of my class to potentially failing out, was a serious issue. My inability to perform basic tac-form was inexcusable. As a result, my case was elevated to the squadron command, and I was left in an anxious limbo, awaiting my fate.

Luckily, my previous high performance earned me a rare third chance. If I failed this time, I faced the bleak prospect of becoming a surface warfare officer (SWO), a miserable soul-crushing fate involving missions like pepper spraying rats while sleep-deprived in the dank hull of a ship. In my view, this was a fate worse than death.

When the flight schedule was posted that evening, I saw that I was paired with an experienced Hornet pilot known for failing struggling students. Nevertheless, I was determined to succeed. I visualized the maneuvers constantly, chair-flying the event repeatedly in my head. My nerves kept sleep at bay, which gave me more time to practice.

I arrived for the flight anxiety-ridden yet as prepared as possible. The instructor grilled me throughout the pre-flight briefing, probing for signs of weakness. Still, I held my own, speaking competently on topics from tac-form to aircraft systems knowledge. His apparent satisfaction with my answers gave me a slight confidence boost, but the real test—performing in the jet—was yet to come.

Walking onto the scorching hot flight line, I felt the Texas sun bearing on us. As the jet's engine spooled to life, sweat poured down my face, only subsiding when the underpowered environmental control system finally kicked in, delivering a much-needed whiff of slightly less hot air and a spittle of condensation. We took off and met the flight lead over the vast Texas desert.

Once in combat spread, I fell into a rhythm. After a few turns, I found myself maintaining my position. My nerves dissipated, replaced by a newfound confidence. Tac-form finally made sense. By the flight's end, I was enjoying myself, having successfully performed every maneuver. The instructor's silence throughout the flight allowed me to think independently. In the debrief, he commended my performance under pressure. I had pulled my flying career out of its tailspin at the last moment, and my fate as a frumpy SWO was averted—for now, at least.

CHAPTER 11

The progression from training flights to landing on an actual, moving aircraft carrier was intense. The stakes had never been higher. Nothing else we learned mattered if we couldn't land on the boat. Field carrier landing practices, or FCLPs, used the IFLOLS system, commonly called "the ball," to visually guide us onto a runway painted to mimic the dimensions of an aircraft carrier. By maintaining an appropriate glide slope, we learned to keep the jet in a safe position for landing. Being too high would result in a missed landing, or "bolter," forcing us to make an embarrassing go-around. On the other hand, coming in too low could result in a ramp strike fatality.

The sunny spring day came for carrier qualifications (CQ) aboard the USS *Bush* off the Jacksonville coast. Instructors were wise enough to avoid riding in our back seat for CQ. Because of the danger, our first time taking a trap would be solo. Even with a clear blue sky and favorable weather, the stakes were high and the margin for error was low. The sight of the aircraft carrier from above was daunting—the moving landing strip was just a tiny, gray speck in a vast, blue sea.

From the overhead break of our four-ship division, I maneuvered the T-45 into a decelerating bank, extending the landing gear and flaps. This was my first time landing with the hook down. On the downwind leg of the pattern, I glanced over my left shoulder to see the ship, now slightly more prominent, tearing through the ocean. I double-checked and then triple-checked my landing checklist. My heart pounded in my chest. I was doing this, for real!

I started my approach turn at what I guessed was the right point for the strong winds and aimed to hit precise altitude checkpoints on my descent. I rolled out on the final approach, somehow on centerline and glide slope. The amber ball of the IFLOLS was just above the green datum lights, indicating I was exactly where I needed to be. Beginner's luck.

The ship grew more prominent as I closed in, time seeming to slow down. Using the throttle, I made slight adjustments to maintain my glide slope, relying on a combination of intuitive feel through the seat of my pants and whatever wisdom passed down from the instructors that managed to stick despite my thick skull. Just before touchdown, I felt the "burble," a turbulent air pocket created by the carrier's superstructure. Despite being buffeted by the turbulence, I managed to stay on the glide slope. As the jet slammed onto the deck, the tailhook snagged a wire, bringing the Goshawk to a jarring halt. The force of the rapid deceleration pushed me forward against my harness, and for a moment, I could barely breathe.

Then, as the deceleration eased, I breathed a huge sigh of relief. I had done it. I had successfully landed a jet on a moving aircraft carrier. The intense feeling of accomplishment was indescribable.

I had no time to savor it. A plane director quickly signaled for me to cut the throttle and guided me out of the landing area to make room for the next student's aircraft, closing in behind me on approach.

The adrenaline had barely begun to fade from my first trap when I was taxiing to the catapult at the front of the carrier. With a quick hand signal, I let the shooter know my fuel state so they could adjust the steam catapult system for my launch. The shooters secured the jet in position and ran a last-second systems check, my heart pounding with anticipation. With a sharp salute, I signaled that I was ready. My hands came off the controls as the jet jolted forward, accelerating from zero to about 160 miles per hour in just two seconds. The intense acceleration pressed me so hard into my seat, I couldn't breathe. Then, just as abruptly as it started, the acceleration eased, and I was flying. The adrenaline rush was intoxicating, better than any high. This was it. This was why I joined the navy.

*   *   *

My on-wing instructor for advanced jet training was a hard-ass US Marine major with the call sign "Fat." He was tall and wiry with a glare that could crush hopes and dreams. It was like being under the watchful eye of an ever-angry Frankenstein. His expectations were unattainable. He made it clear from day one that he would accept nothing less than perfection. Even perfect needed to be better. It was exactly what I needed.

Our first brief together was a disaster. I hadn't emptied the garbage, my whiteboard wasn't up to Fat's standards, and I didn't have a complete set of dry-erase markers. Though the mistakes were minor, they were unacceptable in his book. When asked one of the definitions for the day's lesson topic, I casually stumbled through the answer in my own words. He just stared at me as rage fumed from his intense expression. Fat tore me apart as he demanded that each concept and definition be memorized verbatim. If I couldn't provide the briefing topics precisely and confidently, there was no way I would make it. His criticism stung, but it made me realize that this wasn't just flying. I was training to operate one of the most advanced fighter jets in the world, and there was little room for error, even in the set-up of a briefing room. I was forced to bury my non-conforming, free-spirited disposition to become who I needed to be to survive.

The rigorous advanced phase syllabus covered low-level navigation, bombing, and air combat maneuvering. The stress was constant, but I stayed afloat with my intense preparation. Every debrief was a struggle, with Fat always ready to point out shortcomings. But it was also a powerful motivator. I wanted to prove that I could live up to his lofty expectations.

The day I earned my wings is one I'll never forget. Fat cracked a smile, a genuine, rare grin. He shook my hand and then, as per tradition, sprayed me down with pressurized water in celebration. By the time we made the debrief, he was back to his old self, berating me for not bringing a fresh flight suit. I couldn't help but smile as I stood there dripping and proud. I had done it. I had finally earned my wings of gold.

The winging ceremony commenced for our class, a few less than we started with. The ceremony was a gathering of proud, uniformed figures standing tall and looking every bit the part. Then, there was my family. They stood out among the crowd like hippies at a Nixon campaign rally. My mom was a burst of color in a Ms. Frizzle-style dress. My dad sported bushy side-burns and an outfit that looked more thrift shop special than military chic. With her long, dreadlocked hair and bohemian attire, my sister completed the family picture. Yet their proud smiles were as brilliant as anyone else's.

In their eyes, I saw the culmination of two long years of grueling training. I was no longer just their son or brother; I was a winged naval aviator. The shiny gold insignia on my uniform sparkled in the Texas sun, a symbol of my achievement, my dedication, and the incredible journey I had undertaken.

Fellow aviators punched the wings firmly into my chest until I bled.

And now, another adventure was about to begin. I was bound for Virginia Beach, Virginia, ready to take the skies in the coveted F/A-18 Super Hornet. It was a dream come true, and having my oddball family there to share that moment with me made it all the more memorable.

CHAPTER 12

Stepping into the massive hangar of VFA-106, "the Gladiators," at Naval Air Station Oceana in Virginia Beach was like a dream. The sight of the F/A-18 Super Hornets, hulking and formidable, filled me with awe. I recalled that transitioning from the Cessna 152 puddle jumper to the slightly more robust Cessna 172 Skyhawk was a leap. But this . . . this was a quantum leap.

We started at NAS Oceana with two weeks of computer-based training (CBT). Hours turned into days of screen time, flipping through seemingly endless facts and figures, trivia, and technicalities. The content felt disconnected from the reality of the cockpit. Yet I tried to absorb as much as possible, drinking from the proverbial firehose. The days were long, demanding constant attention to detail, but the buzz of excitement kept me going. When I wasn't studying, I worked out at Valiant Cross-Fit, sampled the refreshingly wide selection of local cuisine, and savored the proximity to the ocean.

Despite the frequent bouts of impostor syndrome, I pushed forward, eager to learn and grow. Robust simulator training began next, where we got to grips with the F/A-18's systems and emergency procedures. It was after one such session that I had an unexpected encounter. A civilian sim operator approached me in the parking lot. With her tight red dress, blonde punk-rock hair, and body tattoos, she was hard to miss among the sea of drab flight suits. After offering me her number with a smile, I quickly recalled my peers' cautionary tale about a similar encounter with her.

A marine aviator had been lured into a rather unconventional situation involving a large dog kennel and a variety of . . . devices, all under the pretense of helping change a light fixture at her house. Semper Fi. His claims of hasty retreat made for an amusing story and helpful, cautionary tale to be wary of the lady in red.

Despite my evasion, I would soon regret not taking up her offer. Her influence stretched beyond her charm to the realm of simulator scheduling, and I found myself paired frequently with the least amiable instructors. The trials I faced in the simulator under their disgruntled gaze were undoubtedly more taxing than any encounter in a woman's boudoir, no matter how exotic.

At VFA-106, our newly minted wings were hardly a source of awe for the RAG (replacement air group) instructors. Most of them had seen combat and completed several sea tours. They were our role models, the epitome of the warriors we aspired to be. As fresh recruits (or "cones," a term I soon discovered was far from a term of endearment), we knew we had much to learn.

The trials and tribulations of the previous years amounted to little in the grand scheme of things. We were back at the bottom, met with disdain and cynicism. It was a never-ending, humbling experience, yet I was prepared to weather whatever storm necessary to earn my place among the ranks of the strike fighter pilots.

However, the adversity seemed to seep deeper, driven by a misguided interpretation of a recently released white paper from the squadron training officer. The paper had been used to fuel a narrative that our millennial generation was full of entitled snowflakes who needed a wake-up call. The irony was not lost on me, as many instructors expressing their disdain were millennials.

As I prepared for my first flight, I leaned on the harsh lessons from Fat. My briefing with Squeezer, my instructor, went smoothly, and soon enough, I was geared up at the controls of the Super Hornet. The jet was a beast, with ground handling more like a tank than any aircraft I'd previously flown. With two massive F414-GE-400 turbofan engines, proper throttle discipline is required during taxiing to avoid destroying something with the powerful jet blast.

Once cleared for takeoff, I guided the aircraft onto the runway and eagerly throttled the engines into maximum afterburner, harnessing the raw power of forty-four thousand pounds of thrust. The acceleration was immediate and forceful, pushing us back into our seats as we rapidly reached rotation speed. A gentle pull on the stick, and we were airborne, the world shrinking beneath us. The Super Hornet was almost too fast for my squirrel brain to keep up. But there was no turning back now. We were in the air, and the journey was only beginning.

Completely silent to this point, Squeezer's calm voice came over the inter-cockpit communication system with a question about our destination. "So, where are we going?" he asked.

Panic set in as I realized that none of the waypoints for our flight had correctly loaded. It was a critical oversight, and I cursed under my breath. But Squeezer, demonstrating his calm demeanor, swiftly entered the coordinates manually to salvage the situation. After I mentally kicked my own ass for making such a stupid mistake, I managed to salvage the flight.

The flight progressed smoothly from there as we engaged in various aerobatic maneuvers to explore the superb handling characteristics. The advanced fly-by-wire flight control system of the Super Hornet made it a joy to handle, and I couldn't help but revel in the sheer thrill of flying such an incredible machine. The weight of constant pressure momentarily melted away, allowing my inner child to soar through the sky. I was living the dream.

Piloting the F/A-18 Super Hornet.

The flight training progressed rapidly, with only a handful of actual flights before my first Super Hornet solo. How the comprehensive naval training had prepared us for this moment was remarkable. Early flights included exhilarating low-level flying, blasting through the Blue Ridge Mountains at breakneck speeds just a few hundred feet above the ground. The speed and intensity of the jet were breathtaking as landscapes flew by in a blur. In these moments, the military's relentless efforts to make everything arduous seemed to dissipate.

CHAPTER 13

Meanwhile, as a single guy in my mid-twenties, I ventured into the Chic's Beach dating scene, hoping to meet someone exceptional or at least attractive. Nights at Chick's Oyster Bar, the infamous watering hole, constantly degraded into more dudes and less space each weekend. A gaggle of belligerent pilots, divers, and SEALs fought over the small handful of single women bold enough to entertain such a disorderly crowd of the navy's finest.

With online dating emerging as the new hotness, I set up a profile. After weeks of lackluster swamp donkeys and battle toads, I finally connected with an attractive match. She met my robust requirements: Her profile picture was stunning and she responded to my messages. We scheduled a date, but she stood me up. Despite her apologies, I was hesitant to give it another try. However, when she messaged me to meet at the King Neptune statue on the Oceanfront, I couldn't resist the temptation, ignoring the warning from my roommate, who, considerably more intelligent than me, sensed something was off with this woman. I should have listened.

The following day, I paced around our agreed meeting spot, half-expecting to be stood up again. But to my surprise, Tiffany emerged from the beachside boardwalk, gracefully bouncing as her jogging pace slowed to a hypnotizing, hip-swaying stroll. The sight of her instantly made my pulse quicken; she was even more stunning in person. Her skin glowed with sparkling beads of sweat as the morning sun cast its warm light upon her. She wore fitted yoga pants and a revealing sports bra, accentuating her athletic build, firm, pierced midriff, and perky curves. An enticing tattoo peeked out just above the waistline on the front of her left hip, which made me even more curious to see just a little lower. Magnetic confidence beamed from her gorgeous brown eyes and perfect white smile. Her presence was commanding, and I couldn't help but be drawn to her. This was the kind of out-of-my-league woman I was used to being ignored by.

As we settled into our conversation, it was effortless, almost as if we had known each other for years. We sat by the ocean, the rhythmic sound of waves setting the perfect backdrop. As we sipped our coffee, I felt wholly entranced by her charisma. She was witty and eloquent, and she carried an air of mystery that made me want to know more. By the time we finished our coffees, I was hooked. We didn't hesitate to set up our next date; I was eager to see her again.

It wasn't long before our chemistry exploded like a blazing supernova. In those early days, Tiffany seemed like everything I had ever dreamed of—adventurous, outgoing, and affectionate. She had a wild side that excited me, a sense of spontaneity that matched my own thirst for life. Our connection felt electric, and the sexual chemistry was nothing short of intoxicating. It was unlike anything I had ever experienced, and I willingly surrendered to the magnetic pull between us.

But the intensity of our attraction clouded my judgment. Within weeks, I found myself daydreaming about introducing her to my friends back in Michigan. I envisioned us laughing around bonfires on the beach, her at my side as I taught her how to kiteboard. I told myself this was more than just infatuation or incredible sex—maybe, just maybe, it was love in its purest form.

Yet beneath the fiery passion, there were moments when a hint of something unsettling flickered in her eyes—something I chose to ignore. But in those initial weeks, I was too captivated to notice the red flags. I was falling hard, and in the heat of the moment, it was easy to overlook the warning signs that hinted at the storm to come.

As our relationship unfolded, Tiffany appeared to be the quintessential partner. However, she requested to meet up one day. Her tone sounded worried, and a pang of anxiety gripped me as I wondered about the impending conversation. The drastic swings between ecstatic highs and dread in our relationship were just beginning.

We met at a nearby beach park. Emerging from her brand-new white Subaru WRX STI—a street-legal rally car I had coveted since childhood—was Tiffany. Much to my surprise, she assisted a toddler out of the back seat. He tottered toward me, her hand in his. With her flawless smile, she introduced him as her son and explained that she wanted to ensure my intentions before introducing him. While her precaution was understandable, her lack of openness left me somewhat unsettled.

Walking the sandy stretch with Tiffany, she narrated a harrowing tale of her past abusive relationship with her son's father, which ultimately compelled her to leave for their safety. I hadn't envisioned taking on a paternal role amidst my rigorous training, yet I was moved by an irresistible urge to shield them. And, of course, my deep feelings for Tiffany lingered. Perhaps I could be their knight in shining armor.

My relationship with Tiffany quickly spiraled into an emotional roller coaster. One moment, our passion blazed like wildfire—the intensity of our connection was undeniable. The sexual chemistry between us was electric, pulling me deeper into her orbit with each encounter. Just the sound she would make with an exhale when excited or a glimpse of her inviting hips swaying in her stylish outfits overwhelmed my primal male systems. But just as I felt securely enveloped in our closeness, she'd suddenly withdraw. The distance was jarring—cold and inexplicable. And yet, before I could make sense of the shift, she would reel me back in, her apologies tender, her words laced with sweetness that made me forget the sting of her previous retreat. Tiffany expertly weaponized her extraordinary sexuality and knew she had me wrapped around her finger.

It was disorienting, like being caught in the pull of opposing currents. One minute, I felt anchored to something real, something meaningful. The next, I was adrift, unsure of where we stood. This constant push and pull wore me down, but I couldn't let go. Not only had I grown fond of Tiffany, but I had also become attached to her little boy. I felt a deep need to be a positive influence in his life, to be the stable figure I imagined he was missing.

Tiffany's stories of her past abusive relationships were harrowing, and I clung to them as justification for her erratic behavior at the time. I convinced myself that I was helping her, that I could be the person who pulled her out of the darkness of her trauma. It anchored me in place, hoping against hope that I could fix what was broken. But each emotional peak and valley in our relationship took its toll. I found myself increasingly exhausted and emotionally drained from the constant highs and lows.

Beneath the surface, though, there was something more sinister brewing—something I couldn't fully grasp then. Tiffany's need for control started to creep into every corner of our relationship. While I thought I was helping her heal, I slowly became entangled in a web she was spinning, unknowingly playing the role she needed me to fulfill. In retrospect, it became clear that her affection wasn't as pure as I had once believed. Her growing reliance on me wasn't just emotional; it was also strategic.

She used me to establish financial security, a safety net to sever ties with her previous relationship. While there were moments when I believed she genuinely cared for me, there was a darker undercurrent to her actions. Tiffany's past trauma had left scars, and those scars manifested in her desire to control every aspect of her life, including me. I didn't realize then that I had become part of her escape plan. She needed a place to land, and I was it.

As time passed, I began to feel the weight of her control. The subtle ways she manipulated situations and the calculated apologies followed by demands became clearer. But by then, I was already deeply invested, not just in her but also in her son. I stayed, clinging to the hope that things would get better if I loved her enough and endured the roller coaster long enough. But deep down, I knew I was losing myself in the process. The stress and poor sleep started taking a toll on my demanding career.

CHAPTER 14

Our RAG class was embarking on the final leg of the fighter phase, and VFA-106 was saddling up for a trip down to Key West. This was the crucible where fighter pilots were truly forged: the infamous Fighter Det, our version of Hell Week. It promised two punishing weeks of a relentless onslaught of grueling briefings, hazardous, high-stress flying, and soul-sapping debriefs—a baptism by fire twice daily.

Air-to-air tactics played out over long ranges, their complex weave both highly technical and bewildering. It was a crucible of decision-making, a gauntlet thrown down to test every ounce of our multitasking ability. Flying in dynamic formation while wrestling with the attack radar's HOTAS control system was like trying to play the world's most challenging video game at a breakneck pace, with lives on the line. All the while, I had to maintain comms, juggling instructions and updates as I maneuvered the aircraft in dynamic tactical formation. The mental and physical strain was unparalleled. But we had a mantra to guide us: form, sensor, comm, a triage of priorities to follow when everything was spiraling out of control. The worst-case scenario wasn't improper radar mechanics or a comms breakdown; it was crashing into my flight lead, another aircraft, or the ground. Staying in position was paramount.

I couldn't control the countless variables I'd encounter in each mind-melting flight, but I could prepare for every brief like I'd be face-to-face with Fat. My ability to articulate the technical subject matter helped compensate for any struggles with practically applying the rapidly expanding tactical skillset.

Fighter Det drew to a close. I was spent, but a sense of accomplishment came with it. This was just the first taste of the demanding life in a fleet squadron, and I was nearly ready for it . . . if I could land the Super Hornet on the boat at night.

*   *   *

The final stretch of the RAG, carrier qualifications (CQ), presented us with our most challenging task yet: nighttime carrier operations. The risks were alarmingly high. A combination of severe weather and nocturnal landings could swiftly spiral into a disastrous situation. As novice pilots, we were exceedingly vulnerable.

A rigorous simulator curriculum precluded the actual aircraft carrier trials. The phantom of possible emergencies loomed large as we maneuvered through complex night carrier approaches in the sim. Concurrently, we spent a month immersed in field carrier landing practice (FCLP), refining our precision for landing on a vessel that swayed and swerved on the boundless sea. Any signs of weakness and the dream of landing on the ship would remain unfulfilled.

This demanding month-long saga brought us face-to-face with the inevitable question: Were we prepared to become genuine tailhook pilots? Nighttime carrier operations were in a league of their own, instilling a sense of dread even in the bravest of cones.

As we set sail, a fading tropical storm forced our carrier qualifications to a halt. The tempest toyed with the gigantic ship like a miniature sailboat in a bath. Simply navigating through the rocking carrier's internal labyrinth of passageways was challenging. How in the hell would we land on this thing in the dark?

As the storm's fury subsided, we manned our jets, returning within the tolerable limits for carrier qualification operations. The oceanic darkness was so dense that I couldn't see my hand in front of me. Stepping onto the pitching deck of the aircraft carrier on that stormy night, I was acutely aware of the perils before me. The chaos, humming propellers, thrashing wires, and the ever-present risk of aircraft collisions all amplified the seriousness of the situation.

Climbing into the cockpit, I mentally prepared myself for my first night trap. However, the stifling fumes from the adjacent Hornet's roaring exhaust made breathing difficult. My eyes burned as tears mixed with the rapidly forming snot dripping into my boat-stache. Symptoms of carbon monoxide poisoning crept over me.

Just as I was about to start the smoke and fume emergency procedure, the plane captain signaled me to begin my taxi. Clear of the pungent vapors, I wiped my face, secured my oxygen mask, and pressed on. The closeness to the deck's edge and the churning dark ocean beneath layered on an additional dose of anxiety.

Perched on the catapult, I readied myself for the impending launch. With the engines rumbling in full afterburner, I braced for the catapult to shoot me into the pitch-black void off the bow. A mistimed launch could hurl me straight into the roiling shadowy waves below. In a blink, I was catapulted from stationary to over 180 miles per hour, the tremendous two-second acceleration pushing me back into my seat.

The sudden force of the launch knocked the chart light loose, rendering it inoperable and engulfing me in darkness.

I had to rely on the cumbersome backup finger light to use my kneeboard, adding an extra hurdle at the worst possible moment. As I ascended, the pervasive darkness swallowed me, with residual tears from the fumes still obscuring my vision.

Upon completing a timing computation and reaching altitude, I initiated my intricate descending arc back to the carrier. Every step of the Case III approach required flawless execution to maintain the pattern's flow of aircraft. Despite coping with the lingering effects of the fumes and the awkward finger light, I focused on my instruments as I neared the carrier. Moments from touchdown, a glowing amber orb broke through the murky darkness. I relayed my ball call to the landing signal officer (LSO) as I transitioned to visual.

"130 Rhino ball, 6.2 Gill," I said.

Cappy's crass voice, the last one I wanted to hear, acknowledged, "Roger ball." My life was now in his hands.

As I was about to touch down, I encountered the burble, the turbulent gust of wind from the control tower, throwing off my precision. Fighting to maintain glide slope at the last second, the Super Hornet's robust landing gear smashed into the coarse steel hard deck and bounded me back into the air. Narrowly missing the wires, I climbed into the wave-off pattern. Fuck.

The unrelenting pressure intensified, knowing I had limited attempts before reaching a bingo fuel state and diverting to NAS Oceana. On each pass, it felt like a force field over the wires repelled my tailhook from connecting as I briefly touched down on the landing area. Instinctively, I throttled forward, propelling myself back into the darkness. Fear had overwhelmed my intuitive feel for the aircraft. After narrowly missing the wires a few more times, I had no option but to raise my gear and flaps and reroute to the shore on a bingo profile.

The lonely flight of disgrace back to Oceana was profoundly demoralizing as I traversed the pitch-black chasm through the heart of the ominous rainclouds. The only light was the dim green glow of my heads-up display (HUD) reflecting off my glazed eyes. Failing to qualify that night weighed heavily on me. Landing a jet on a moving ship amid stormy, pitch-black conditions was the ultimate test for a pilot, and I had failed.

Late that restless night, I wallowed in despair, wrestling with self-doubt. Despite the demoralizing setback, I resolved to press on. Struggling during night CQ was a common occurrence. If luck favored me, I may get another chance.

A small, informal review board comprising instructor pilots and a flight surgeon convened to evaluate my potential for another attempt at the boat. After conversing with me and reviewing my aviation training records, they assessed whether I was in the right frame of mind and trainable enough for a second shot. Despite my fair share of struggles in flight training, I always mustered a positive attitude and moved forward. No matter how adept a pilot is, everyone falters in the dynamic world of naval aviation. Bouncing back from such profound failure is a potent virtue. The board decided to give me a second chance, but the relief from this good news was quickly overshadowed by the daunting reality of having to face night carrier operations again. There wouldn't be another opportunity if I didn't qualify this time.

I rolled from my original class, now celebrating its graduation, and joined the next group as they began their month-long CQ curriculum. Repeating the sims and FCLPs gradually helped rebuild my confidence. Predictably, Cappy was the head LSO for the upcoming CQ det.

Behind the boat, I applied the lessons from my subtle errors and overcame the nervous energy that led to my initial failure.

Daytime carrier operations went smoothly. As the sun disappeared over the expansive sea, I mentally prepared for the night. On my first pass with the hook down, I felt the burble push me off course seconds before touchdown. I rode the wave this time and remained focused in the crucial last seconds. As my jet impacted the deck forcefully, the tailhook snagged a massive steel cable. The sudden deceleration pushed me forward in the harness. I had never been so thrilled to feel the wind knocked out of my lungs. I finally had my first night trap. After nine more passes in the punchy pitch-black night, I qualified. A month of tension dissipated as I savored my midrats breakfast burrito below deck in celebration.

CHAPTER 15

After obtaining my carrier qualifications in the Super Hornet, I graduated from training at VFA-106. At the patching ceremony, I eagerly awaited joining a fleet squadron as a navy strike fighter pilot; it was a moment of sheer elation. I embarked on a new career chapter as a navy strike fighter pilot with VFA-143. It was a significant milestone, and I was determined to live up to the legacy of the World-Famous Pukin' Dogs and make the squadron proud—or so I hoped.

After three and a half years of toil, the euphoria of reaching my goal was something, but the brutal truth soon dawned: I didn't know jack shit. Keeping a low profile, I dedicated myself to relentless study and practice sessions. I consistently chair flew each mission, visualizing flight maneuvers with my eyes closed, my makeshift simulator. I made up for what I lacked in academic prestige with hard work.

I had luck, being assigned to the Pukin' Dogs, a team of stellar chaps. Their moniker for the FNGs (Fuckin' New Guys) was Poop, the most worthless part of the dog. I came on board alongside another rookie just as the squadron returned from two consecutive deployments. After several months at sea, the raunchy catchphrase "Tongue punch to the fart box" had been a point of interest in the ready room during the squadron's journey back from the Persian Gulf. They called us Tongue Punch and Fart Box to mark our initiation. Irrespective of our near-worthless status, we were gradually embraced by the seasoned combatants as part of their brotherhood. After more than three years in the navy, the senior pilots had finally recognized us as at least partially human, regardless of our position at the lowest rung of the ladder.

*   *   *

The squadron VFA-143, originally known as "the Griffins" in the 1950s, had its name switched generations before my arrival. At a squadron party in the officer's club, the commanding officer's wife noticed a drooping, homemade paper-mache statue of the squadron's mascot, a griffin. Looking at the sad creation, she drawled in her heavy Southern accent, "That looks like a pukin' dawg." The name, as you might guess, stuck.

I had the naive assumption that being a fighter pilot was primarily about flying, but the reality in the US Navy is quite different. Most of the day was swallowed by an array of ground jobs, collateral duties, and an excessive amount of mandatory online learning not related to flying that bordered on the meaningless.

As Poop, I was a ripe target for the roving task-by-scan eyeballs of the department heads who were always looking for minions to carry out their bidding. Studying and flight preparation were afterthoughts squeezed into whatever free time I could find. There was no shirtless volleyball in the afternoon sun. However, reaching my dream made the grind of endless ground duties bearable.

I found little room for complaint when I observed the backbreaking labor the maintainers poured into keeping our jets airborne. Us pilots had the privilege of mandatory crew rest on flying days to rejuvenate our strength. But those stout-hearted enlisted endured the grind with grit, day in and day out. Their unwavering commitment was the backbone of our operations. Yet their accolades were often a fraction of the recognition they deserved.

*   *   *

During my time with the Pukin' Dogs, the prevailing stalemate among US government leadership weighed heavily on the servicemembers. As a country, we are all on the same side, yet the constant discord even impeded consensus on an issue as vital as the military budget time and time again. I observed some of the corrosive aftermath firsthand.

The continuing resolution (CR) bills were a specific case in point, causing an alarming degree of wastage. Like a festering bandage, these bills dictated that the same funding allocated in the previous year could only be utilized for identical items and amounts in the current year. So, suppose a squadron received a million-dollar budget for office equipment last year. In that case, they'd have the same allocation this year, regardless of need. This earmarked funding could only be used for that specific purpose, leading to absurd situations where, out of fear of permanently losing future funding, squadrons would buy surplus computers and desks only to stow them away unused. Meanwhile, the urgent million-dollar components necessary to keep an aircraft airborne received no funding.

The outcome was grim. Dozens of F/A-18s were in disrepair across NAS Oceana, corroding on the flight line, awaiting the necessary parts. The base's leaky, outdated hangars shed asbestos in their desperate need for new roofs, leading to long-term, costlier damage. Funds for essential maintenance were so severely curtailed that the grass was allowed to grow rampant, causing a rapid surge of servicemembers hospitalized for venomous snake bites. Upon visiting to assess the state of the hangars, an experienced contractor commented that he hadn't seen such dilapidated structures since his involvement in salvage operations after the collapse of the Soviet Union. The "tactical hard deck" policy slashed each pilot's flying time to a scant fifteen hours per month, leading to a precarious decline in proficiency. And with diminished proficiency came an upsurge in costly mishaps.

Despite the Department of Defense's hearty budget, the domineering influence of the defense industry has resulted in a disparity between advancing new technologies and maintaining the servicemembers and equipment we already have. While the defense industry flourishes, perpetuating unending global conflicts, soldiers are sent into high-intensity urban combat with antiquated, duct-taped, Vietnam-era weapons and without body armor. Jets decay on the flight line while our hangars crumble.

Personnel retention continues to decline as our service members are forced to carry the extra burden born of chronic understaffing. The squadrons are hemorrhaging experience. Our commanding officers and the upper echelons of military leadership are left powerless to rectify known issues, held hostage by the policies dictated by a government leadership increasingly disconnected from the realities on the ground. The continuing gridlock in the halls of Washington further fractures our nation with each passing day. It's my fervent hope that we, as a nation, can rediscover common ground before our adversaries further seize the opportunity to take advantage of us—if we don't implode first. Rant complete.

*   *   *

While the majority of the flights remained graded, as pilots progressed through the stringent TOPGUN Strike Fighter Weapons and Tactics syllabus to attain combat wingman, section lead, and division lead qualifications, we were occasionally offered what we affectionately called "good deal" flights.

One of the most thrilling flights I participated in with the Pukin' Dogs was alongside another junior officer, Mitch, short for Man Bitch. Two twenty-somethings were entrusted with one of the most technologically advanced aircraft ever designed. They granted the liberty to roar through the afternoon, lacerating the sky over the Blue Ridge Mountains during a low-level flight.

VFA-143 Pukin' Dogs circa 2014.

The experience was nothing short of extraordinary. We were engaged in a high-speed chase, pursuing each other at neck-breaking speeds of over five hundred miles per hour.

The snowcapped peaks served as our playground, and we skimmed above them, just a few hundred feet above the ground. This proximity to the earth renders an ineffable perception of the speed you're moving.

Following a brief stopover at the marine air base in Cherry Point for refueling, we burst over the Atlantic, ready for gloves-off, high-aspect BFM. On our return, we indulged in the sheer joy of cloud surfing. The radiant cumulus clouds, lit by the late afternoon sun, offered a near-surreal backdrop as I chased Mitch's jet through the towering formations, imagining them as a snowcapped dreamscape.

On another memorable good deal sortie, I found myself thrust into a CAS rehearsal, training with Navy SEALs, backed by a pair of agile Little Birds from the 160th Special Operations Aviation Regiment (SOAR), the army's primo spec-ops helicopter unit. The training mission pulled no punches, a true mirror of the challenges we would meet in an active war zone. The warriors we trained with were barely dusted off from the sandstorm before they were thrust back into the Middle East. I foresaw joining them soon, providing CAS from the sky as my air wing was gearing up to deploy to the same volatile region.

The SOAR's Little Birds moved with deadly precision, ferrying the SEALs to their simulated battlefield. As the SEALs launched their assault on a high-value target in the mock village, my flight lead and I swooped in overhead to provide armed overwatch, using our ATFLIRs to cut through the night. We released our laser-guided training rounds at the command "cleared hot" from the SEAL JTAC, a rock-steady voice over the radio. The Little Birds let loose a controlled chaos of minigun and rocket fire that lit up the twilight.

The SEAL JTAC seamlessly orchestrated air strike after air strike, and the Little Birds and our pair of Pukin' Dog Super

Hornets delivered a choreographed display of force as we received the go-ahead time after time. As the sun dipped below the horizon, the sky was set ablaze with the flash of the Little Birds' miniguns and rockets. This spectacle could outshine any Hollywood sci-fi blockbuster. Amid the frenzy, I realized how incredibly fortunate I was to be in this place, doing this job, even if tonight was training. This is what it must be like to be a fire-breathing dragon.

These flights taught me the most and pushed me to do my best. The pressure, the unrelenting demands, the never-ending grind—they all melted away on days like these. Regardless of the ongoing geopolitical disasters, the sentiment was shared amongst the squadron. The opportunity to back warriors of this caliber in the crucible of combat was a privilege borne with pride.

CHAPTER 16

Tiffany's emotional swings worsened as I began to find my rhythm within the squadron, juggling flying duties, various ground responsibilities, and collateral duties. She picked up on my growing concerns as our passion began to wane.

After a long day in the squadron, I showered at her place while she bathed her son in a separate bathtub. She surprisingly handed me the bubble-ensconced boy before I could grab a towel. I awkwardly held him as she hastily took several photos of us, assuring me they were innocuous face shots. But when I reached for her phone to check, sensing something was off, she pulled away, deflecting with a subject change. A worm of suspicion began to gnaw at me. Many pieces of her stories were no longer adding up. The effects of her sex appeal on my dumb ass had been very influential, but she could sense me starting to distance myself. Though she never fully shared her darker childhood traumas, I suspected she struggled with her mental health due to sexual abuse at a young age. Having experienced my mental health challenges during high school, I wanted to help, but things started to get violent.

One night, while her boy was with his father, I noticed Tiffany quickly wash down some pills with a beer. When confronted about the drugs, she explained them as sleep medication, citing some recent struggles with insomnia. As I turned my attention back to the ongoing painting project of my rental, Tiffany spiraled into an alarming descent.

With the combination of mystery pills and alcohol kicking in, she initiated a barrage of unprovoked rude comments that swiftly degenerated into an aggressive tirade. Anticipating her unpredictable behavior, I discreetly hid her keys when she decided to head to a bar. Her response was a violent outburst, but her petite frame and drug-induced clumsiness made it easy for me to avoid serious harm.

After a solid hour of her berating me incoherently, I'd had enough; I revealed where her keys were hidden. In a fury, she snatched them up. She stormed out, speeding into the night in her street-legal rally car, sporting expired temporary plates. As the sound of her turbocharged engine receded, I secured the house and turned off the lights.

About fifteen minutes later, the distinct hiss of her turbocharger signaled her return. Peering out the window, I noted the smashed front of her new car. I retreated as she pulled into the driveway and commenced an incessant doorbell ringing. I hastily located a dishtowel to jam into the doorbell, silencing it.

As the bell's ringing ceased, Tiffany took to pounding on the door while hurling insults at me. After a few minutes, silence took over, giving me hope that she'd exhausted herself. That hope shattered when the sound of breaking glass echoed through the house. My living room window was the first to go, a brick crashing onto the old wooden floor. Stunned, I watched as Tiffany, fury personified, ripped more bricks from the walkway, launching them through each window in the house, one after another. Circling to the back of the house, she flung another through the bedroom window. As I flicked on the light, I saw her clambering through the broken window barefoot, heedlessly trampling over shards of glass, her rage rendering her oblivious to the cuts on her feet.

Now in the kitchen, Tiffany snatched up a stainless steel chef's knife and charged at me, a demonic fury in her eyes. She aimed the blade at my face, but I caught her wrist, prying the knife from her hand. Once disarmed, I wrestled her to the ground, but Tiffany thrashed about, hurling curses and spittle at me. I tried to soothe her, but she wrenched free, grabbing a shard of broken glass. She made a desperate attempt to slash at her wrist, but I was able to disarm her once again. She was pinned on the living room couch, sobbing and pleading for me to let her end her life. She seemed possessed, and I considered whether she needed an exorcism or an ambulance. I could not reach my phone for fear she'd try to harm herself or me if I released her.

Throughout the night, I stayed by her side. Every time she seemed to drift off to sleep, she'd suddenly jerk awake, reaching for more shards of glass. This grueling cycle continued until dawn. As the first rays of sunlight peeked through the smashed windows, she finally fell into an exhausted slumber. The floor was strewn with broken glass, bricks, and debris; every window was shattered. I had to prepare for work.

As I navigated the minefield of debris to make breakfast, Tiffany entered the kitchen, looking confused. I explained her actions from the previous night as gently as I could. She looked shocked, promising to cover the damages. She seemingly had no memory of the violence. I didn't care about the money or the mess; I had worked hard in my military flying career to make it where I was. Coping with her instability was taking a toll on me. I needed to get out of our relationship. With this thought, I headed to the squadron, doing my best to compartmentalize the night's events.

When I returned home that evening, the glass had been cleared away, and the bricks were back in the walkway. Tiffany was still there. I managed to ask her to collect her things calmly. As I asked her to leave, Tiffany alternated between despair and rage. In one moment, she would look at me with those familiar, innocent eyes that had drawn me in, as if part of her was trapped and pleading for me to save her. But when I remained firm in my decision, her rage returned. She began yanking pictures from the wall, smashing them onto the floor. More shattered glass. I watched her calmly, but my lack of reaction seemed to infuriate her further. As she continued to destroy my home, I finally did what I should have done much earlier. I pulled out my phone and dialed 911.

As I waited for the police, Tiffany's mood shifted to remorse, tears streaming down her face as she begged for forgiveness. Despite the damage, I felt sympathetic. Watching someone I had been so close to struggling like this was not what I wished for her. I wanted the woman I fell for back, but she had become more than a distraction. I was on the receiving end of an abusive relationship. A female law enforcement officer arrived not a moment too soon. I explained the situation to her: I wanted Tiffany out of my house, but she refused to leave. The officer had experience with this kind of situation. After much persuasion from the officer, Tiffany finally walked into the neighborhood in tears.

However, the relief was short-lived. Less than an hour after the police departed, Tiffany returned, claiming she wanted to collect her belongings. She apologized again, promising to pay for the broken windows and picture frames. Reluctantly, I let her in to gather her things. I just wanted to let her down easy. After collecting the last of her things, she finally left my rental.

By the end of the week, the broken windows had been repaired. Tiffany texted me asking if I could come and say goodbye to her son. When I kept my distance, she pressured me with subtle threats. It became clear that if I didn't re-engage with her, she could accuse me of sexually assaulting her and her son. The memory of the awkward photograph she'd taken flashed in my mind. I suspect she may have been planning this to keep me in her grasp. With the height of the #MeToo movement, I was acutely aware of the damage an accusation could do, regardless of validity. Being a man disqualified me from due process should such allegations arise. A sense of dread enveloped me. I felt trapped.

I tried to think of a way out of this situation without destroying my life. But the fear of what Tiffany might do kept me silent. Like a stubborn bastard, I could not ask for help, wanting to deal with the quagmire myself. I turned up at work daily, putting on a facade of normalcy. I compartmentalized to perform at the high levels required day in and day out.

An unsettling invasion of black mold forced me to abandon my rental house. Underneath the layer of fresh paint, shadowy clusters of rapidly proliferating fungi began to appear. The sickening scent of toxic mildew was becoming unbearable. A mold specialist, upon inspection, confirmed that the property was infested with countless harmful spores. The subsequent dispute with the property management company left me without a roof over my head as I wrestled with reclaiming my security deposit and canceling the lease. Tiffany, seizing the opportunity, proposed I temporarily lodge with her until I found a new place. Caught in a bind, I agreed.

The evening of January 14, 2014, marked another escalation in the chaos. Tiffany locked herself in her bathroom in an irrational tantrum. Through the door, I could hear the rattle of a pill bottle. Shortly after, in between sobs, she claimed to have swallowed an entire bottle of sleeping meds. Upon arrival, the first responders talked with Tiffany through the locked door. After some time, she admitted she hadn't taken any medications. Once the dust settled, they left. Exhausted, I tried to get some rest. I had a flight the next day—a flight poised to shift my life's trajectory irreversibly.

CHAPTER 17

January 15, 2014, rose cold and crystal clear over Virginia Beach. As I joked with Fisty, we shared a moment of light-hearted banter, conjuring up mental images of Mary Lee, the infamous Great White shark, lurking beneath the icy waves. Given the chilling temperatures and shark-infested waters, it would be a terrible day to eject.

That afternoon, Diego—my seasoned flight lead—and I were nearly complete in a session of high-aspect BFM. We geared up for our final bout of engagement, but our fuel tanks were low, signaling the urgency to return to base. Positioned wing to wing a mile abeam, Diego kicked off the fight, his voice firm across the comms, "Three, two, one, fight's on." I echoed the rallying call, "Fight's on," across our tactical frequency, our jets charging each other with unyielding resolve.

The deafening roar of the jet's thrust reverberated in my ears, catapulting my aircraft with a force that had us crossing paths at the merge in seconds. Partially inverted and nose-low, I continued my descent, pulling the Super Hornet into a teeth-clenching seven-and-a-half-g dive toward the ocean. Abruptly, as my jet passed bullseye nose low, the gravitational pull on my body slackened ominously. The Super Hornet had stopped responding to my commands.

My options for troubleshooting were dwindling as swiftly as the ocean was closing in. I slammed back the throttles and extended the speed brake in a panicked attempt to slow the jet's terrifying descent, but the view in front of me was increasingly consumed by the rapidly closing surface of the ocean. Bitchin' Betty blared, "Pull up. Pull up." *I'm already pulling up! I can't pull up any further!* The ground rush was overwhelming. Time appeared to halt, and a chilling terror seized me. A collision with the ocean was imminent.

In the last possible moments—two seconds from impacting the frigid Atlantic at the speed of sound, 51 degrees nose low, a scant two thousand feet above the surface, barreling through the air at an astonishing 695 miles per hour—I braced for impact as I yanked the black- and yellow-striped ejection handle between my legs.

Even under ideal circumstances—below two hundred knots, flying straight and level—ejecting is perilous. Even controlled ejections can permanently damage a pilot's spine and cause flail injuries to the extremities. I was far beyond the parameters considered survivable, but there were no alternatives in the seconds the situation unfolded. The fact that this was the first high-speed ejection involving the bulky JHMCS helmet was an additional risk that nearly ripped my head off. It was either a certain death in the jet or a slim chance of survival with a transonic ejection. There was no time for contemplation.

In less than half a second, a rocket under my seat ignited, subjecting me to an instantaneous fifty g's of force that compressed my spine like an empty beer can as the canopy was blown clear, followed by fourteen sustained g's as I departed the jet like the Rocketeer. Traveling at 95 percent of the speed of sound at 604 knots indicated airspeed, I lost consciousness as I was torn apart like a ragdoll in a tornado. The force impacting the sound barrier was nearly a hundred times stronger than a Category 1 hurricane.

My helmet ripped off, smashing my skull into the seat and leaving my face unprotected as it slammed into the sound barrier. My neck broke from the extreme whiplash and compression. Both humerus bones in my upper arms shattered from the violent flailing, and my right humerus tore through the brachial artery, causing internal bleeding. My left forearm shattered and severed the median nerve controlling my hand. The steel toes of my boots transformed into wrecking balls and crushed my lower legs. Pieces of tibia fell out, chumming the waters for Mary Lee.

Shark wrangler Jody Whitworth tagging the massive Mary Lee. After a career of researching sharks, Mary Lee remains the second largest white shark Jody's ever tagged, weighing in at 3,500 pounds and measuring sixteen feet long.

The parachute opened just enough to avoid fatal impact with the ocean, but the landing was far from gentle. Hitting the Atlantic's icy 37-degree Fahrenheit water, it swiftly filled my tattered dry suit. My consciousness ebbed in and out, with occasional snapshots of the horrific ordeal. The water felt like countless needles piercing my skin, and the cold was so intense that it gave me an immediate, shocking brain freeze. Having saved my life moments earlier, the parachute was now threatening it, filling with water and dragging me beneath the churning waves.

Devices on the parachute harness, known as SEWARS, are designed to automatically disconnect the parachute risers when submerged in salt water. One of my SEWARS fired but failed to disconnect. The other malfunctioned entirely, not igniting at all. Incapable of manually disconnecting the parachute risers due to my severely damaged arms, I was at the mercy of the ocean. As the canopy sank beneath the rough sea, it repeatedly dragged me under. My lungs were desperately craving air, and the terror was overwhelming. Involuntarily, I inhaled salt water. Everything went black.

*   *   *

Meanwhile, Diego, spotting my parachute, quickly took on the role of on-scene commander, dropping a GPS mark for my location and commencing coordination of the rescue effort with the scant fuel left in his jet. A fishing vessel approximately a mile away caught his eye, and he attempted to contact them via the emergency maritime guard frequency. When the crew failed to respond, Diego flew low and thumped their bow to catch their attention. Once communication was established, he relayed my approximate location. The fishermen had been unaware of the catastrophe despite a fighter jet disintegrating at a near-sonic speed less than a mile away. There was no explosion, no loud noise, just an aircraft that seemingly evaporated. The most prominent pieces of the jet remaining were no bigger than a smashed license plate.

With fuel levels critically low, Diego enacted a "bingo" fuel profile, a direct course to NAS Oceana, handing over the rescue coordination to air traffic control (ATC). Some other nearby Hornet pilots, Bish and Kelvin, established and maintained an overhead vigil on my position using their long-range FLIR cameras. All they could see was a faint glimmer of jet fuel dissolving into the dark blue sea.

The airwaves crackled with the sounds of coordinated efforts to save my life. AC1 Hercules expertly led the rescue coordination via ATC. Sparkles, the standing squadron duty officer (SDO) at VFA-106, and Fisty, the SDO at VFA-143, coordinated the rescue effort. The word of my ejection over the radio hit Fisty like a punch to the gut. Just an hour ago, we had been joking about getting eaten by the massive white shark, now circling near my bleeding body. The Coast Guard station at Elizabeth City was alerted, as were several other nearby vessels and aircraft.

Fortuitously, my life preserver unit (LPU) automatically inflated around my neck, giving me enough buoyancy to bob to the surface occasionally. Each time, I managed to cough out some seawater and gasp in a breath before being dragged back under by my tangled parachute. My consciousness ebbed and flowed. I was shocked that the great white, Mary Lee, hadn't finished me off yet. Chilling imagery from the movie *Jaws* flashed across my mind. Pure dread engulfed me as I was held beneath the surface, involuntarily inhaling salt water, my lungs spasming. In just moments, my dream had transformed into a nightmare.

An HSC-28, H-60 Seahawk helicopter, initially departing from Naval Station Norfolk for a training mission, promptly diverted to my location upon receiving the Mayday call. Joey, the helicopter crew chief, hastily shoved his meatball and marinara sub into a wrapper, tossing it into a corner of the helicopter cabin to prepare for my rescue.

Only a week prior, the onboard rescue swimmer, Cheech, had been involved in another rescue when a large US Navy MH-53E Sea Dragon helicopter crashed due to an onboard fire. While most of the crew survived the initial crash, they succumbed to hypothermia, exacerbated by the navy's policy to place crash survivors on a backboard to prevent aggravating spinal injuries, which unfortunately increased their exposure to the cold water. Coming off a harrowing week, Cheech nevertheless suited up for the cold and prepared to rescue me from the tumultuous ocean without hesitation.

An H-60 Seahawk helicopter from HS-11, stationed on a nearby aircraft carrier, was en route to my position. The fishing vessel that Diego had contacted arrived first. The fishermen threw a rope out to me, but my incapacitated state made it impossible to grab hold. The rope became entangled in the paracord surrounding me like a net of tendrils. While they couldn't pull me aboard, the fishing vessel at least provided a rough visual location of my position. The beacon on my gear had malfunctioned, and without the fishing vessel's proximity, I would have been lost as the ocean currents swept me away from my initial point of entry. The scene was chaotic. As the salt water filled my exhausted lungs, death swallowed me.

*   *   *

Born of a Gaelic myth lives the legacy of my name, Kegan, a tale soaked in the salt of the sea. This is a story not of a man but of a soul in the form of a fisherman wrestling with the tempest's tantrums.

Once a beacon of resolute strength, his vessel was torn apart by the capricious sea's mirth. Stranded in the wild waters, alone but for the primal rage of the storm, he awaited his watery demise, his soul set to be stolen by the sea.

Yet just as despair sought to claim his spirit, a phantom of the deep rose to his aid. A selkie, graced with a sense of destiny, darted through the chaos, defying the storm's tyranny.

Kegan was pulled from the jaws of defeat, the sea's vengeance denied by this mythical creature of the deep. As the shore's safety embraced him, the selkie's seal form shifted, the ocean's illusion dispelled. From a creature of silk and sea, she transformed into a gorgeous woman, a radiant figure carved by the ocean's chisel.

A love as fierce as the storm they'd survived ignited between them. She was the siren to his sailor, the lighthouse to his lost ship, and the calm to his storm.

In Gaelic, Kegan is an ode to passion, a ball of fire lighting the night's darkness. And so, this tale weaves a tapestry of love and resilience, a testament to the heart's unfathomable depths. Echoed in each wave's crest, even the cruel sea can breed a love as enduring as the tides.

*　　*　　*

HS-11's helicopter arrived overhead first. Their capable rescue swimmer leaped into the ocean, but miscommunication and cold water shock led him to believe I was on the fishing vessel, and he swam past me. If HS-11 had retrieved me first, I likely would have died. Unaware of the severity of my injuries, they had orders to fly me back to the aircraft carrier, which was ill-equipped to handle such severe trauma.

HSC-28's crew slowed nearby, vigilantly scanning the scene of the crash. It had been over ninety minutes of struggling for breath. The keen Seahawk pilot managed to spot my head briefly surfacing and maneuvered the helicopter overhead into a hover. With the harsh lessons of the previous week fresh in his mind, Cheech plunged into the near-freezing water.

He swam up to me and submerged to connect to the titanium carabiner on my harness. Once linked, the parachute dragged us both beneath the surface. Despite Cheech's best efforts to swim upward, the ocean currents pulled us down as if tethered to a seabag of cement blocks. Even for a seasoned rescue swimmer like Cheech, the sight of being dragged into the deep blue abyss tangled in paracord was alarming. Relying on his training and experience, Cheech cut the entangled parachute cords and hauled us back to the surface. Aware of the hypothermia threat, Cheech opted to hoist me into the helicopter without a backboard. As we ascended, the rotor wash pelted us, and we spun rapidly. Inside the cabin, Joey and the crew pulled me in. Despite being in shock, I was intermittently conscious.

Once aboard, the helicopter made a beeline for Norfolk General Hospital, a Level I trauma center within reach. The flight took less than an hour, but it felt like five for the crew as I hovered on the brink of life and death, cycling in and out of consciousness. I teetered on the edge of death as the crew applied various resuscitation techniques. My vision dimmed, then went black. A firm sternum rub brought me back to semi-consciousness, my eyes flickering open as I cried out for help, delusional from shock. My physical body was there, but my mind was elsewhere. My behavior oscillated between panicked, disoriented shouting for help and a deathlike stillness.

Joey's meatball sub had escaped its wrapper. By the time we neared the hospital, I was covered in marinara sauce and chunks of tasty ground meat. While I was undoubtedly losing a substantial amount of blood, Joey's lunch remains made my situation appear even more gruesome.

After a flight that took approximately forty-five minutes, the Seahawk landed on the helipad at Sentara Norfolk General Hospital. As hospital staff and the HSC-28 crew moved me onto a gurney, Joey explained my medical status and mentioned that the marinara sauce and ground meat were remnants of his lunch. My left forearm, with its shattered radius and ulna, flopped unnaturally as I was moved. A local news crew filmed me being wheeled into the trauma center, where I continued to sit up and scream for help despite having no memory of doing so.

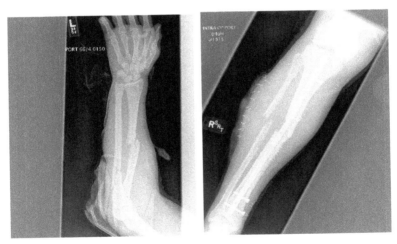

X-rays of just a few of my ten different broken bones.

The talented medical staff sprang into action to save me once I was in the hospital. My core body temperature had plummeted to 87 degrees Fahrenheit, a mere degree away from certain death. Strangely, the severe hypothermia that nearly killed me also saved my life. Had my dry suit not been torn open, I would have bled out from my torn brachial artery and open leg fractures. The hypothermia had constricted blood flow from my extremities to conserve warmth in my vital organs. The cold water was likely beneficial for my brain injury as well. Medical staff raised my core body temperature using convective heat and removed salt water from my lungs. Due to the extensive tissue damage, my kidneys began to fail due to rhabdomyolysis. They put me on IV fluids and administered a blood transfusion.

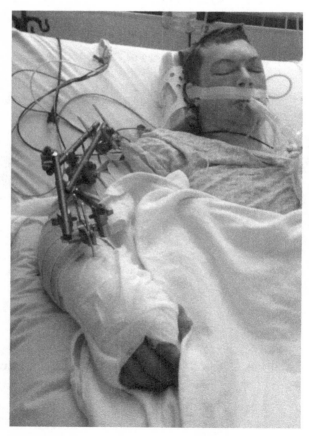

Intubated and comatose following numerous trauma surgeries.

Once somewhat stabilized, I was placed into an induced coma and whisked into surgery. Luckily, a dream team of surgeons was on duty. I suffered from compartment syndrome due to extensive fractures and tissue damage in all four extremities. My limbs were swelling to the point where the circulation was cut off as the surrounding fascia tissue constricted the injured muscle. Without blood flow, the limb would die. In the past, this would have been treated with amputation. Thankfully, a complex limb salvage procedure called fasciotomy is now commonly used in trauma patients, which saved me from potential quadriplegia. The surgeons carefully cut open my skin to expose the fascia. They then cut open the fascia around the damaged muscles on the sides of my legs and arms to relieve the pressure from inflammation. This procedure requires considerable skill and experience to avoid damaging nerves and blood vessels. Thankfully, it was successful and allowed blood to start circulating again.

Over the following week, I underwent over a dozen surgical procedures. The surgeons rebuilt my skeleton with titanium intramedullary rods, screws, and surgical-grade steel plates. Interestingly, the evolution of this treatment can be traced back to World War II.

Luftwaffe pilots often suffered from broken legs after being shot down. In inhumane experimental surgeries performed on prisoners, surgeons discovered a method to rebuild broken legs by screwing metal plates onto the outside of the legs and into the bone. Although the pilots had to be wheelchaired to the aircraft, they could fully operate their aircraft, including the rudder pedals, once strapped in.

Over time, the procedure evolved to involve inserting intramedullary rods, or "nails," into the core of a broken long bone to salvage breaks that were previously too damaged to heal. Both my humeri in my upper arms and the tibias in my lower legs had titanium nails inserted and held in place with screws. My left forearm was reconstructed with a surgical-grade steel plate and several screws. A large metal external fixator temporarily held my right arm into place. My X-rays could be mistaken for Wolverine's from *X-Men*.

After several operations, I lay comatose in the intensive care unit (ICU) when an attentive nurse discovered my right hand was unnaturally cold and beginning to turn blue. Within hours, I was back in the operating room, this time for a vein graft to mend my torn brachial artery. The surgical team removed a section of a vein from elsewhere in my body and repurposed it to reestablish blood flow to my arm and hand via the brachial artery. This successful procedure staved off the need to amputate my right hand. Despite being still unconscious, I clung to life.

Upon my induction into VFA-143, I filled out a form detailing who should be contacted in case of an emergency. That form had been sealed and kept with my commanding officer. Upon unsealing the envelope, Diego found the name of my friend Matt, with whom I had coached kiteboarding. Matt had been like a brother to me, possessing the relaxed demeanor and inherent leadership abilities necessary in such a crisis. When he answered Diego's call and was informed about the situation, he exclaimed, "Scrappy? You mean Scrappy?" The nickname "Scrappy" had stuck, and Diego found it fitting enough to share with the squadron.

I remained in an induced coma for a week and underwent numerous surgical procedures. Despite several attempts to wake me, I remained unconscious and was transferred to the ICU at Naval Hospital Portsmouth. My parents had flown in and were in the hospital waiting room, along with several pilots from my squadron and friends from flight school. The mood was somber, my fate hanging in the balance. Yet the revelation of my nickname, Scrappy, seemed to lighten the mood somewhat. A squadron mate chimed in, "He's a scrappy motherfucker. He'll be OK." His words brought laughter to the room, and the quick-witted members of the Pukin' Dogs soon abbreviated "scrappy motherfucker" to "Smurf." I finally had a call sign.

Of course, to circumvent the politically correct climate in the military, every non-PC call sign requires a cover story. In the eyes of the navy, I officially became Smurf because I was a short guy who had turned blue from hypothermia.

CHAPTER 18

My first memory of waking up was a blend of familiar voices and the smell of disinfectant. As I slowly opened my eyes, I was met with the sight of family, friends, and Tiffany crowding around me. Everyone was overjoyed to see me awake. My mom's face was wet with tears of relief. Awaking felt like emerging from a deep slumber. I recognized familiar faces but was disoriented, unable to recall why I found myself in a brightly lit hospital room. My body was encased in vacuum-sealed plastic to prevent infection, and hundreds of stitches and staples delineated the surgical wounds on my arms and legs. My skin looked thin and pallid, and I felt like a character in a zombie movie.

I was unable to move the thin wool blanket covering me. The trauma had left me paralyzed. The irritation in my throat was due to the recently removed ventilator tube, and my chest was covered with sticky pads connected to machines monitoring my vital signs. Yet I was surprisingly pain-free, courtesy of the fentanyl being steadily infused into my IV.

I pleaded with my squadron mates to bring me a wheelchair and let me leave the hospital. There was so much work I needed to catch up on. One of my weightlifting buddies from OCS stifled a laugh as he gently told me, "You're going to be here for a while, dude." I'm grateful for my countless hours lifting weights with him during flight school. That extra muscle mass had played a role in my survival. I had yet to comprehend the full scope of my injuries and the long road ahead.

The brutal reality of my situation was brought home by the medical team. The overworked staff explained the severity of my injuries from the high-speed ejection, informing me that I would likely never walk or use my arms again and that my flying career was over. Their prognosis was crushing, but I decided to push back instead of succumbing to despair. If you want a fighter pilot to do something, tell them it's impossible. My only thought was, *Fuck that! I can't wait to prove you all wrong.* I was determined to forge a new daily mission centered on making whatever progress I could, regardless of how small it might seem.

Sure, I couldn't sit up, but I could try to wiggle my hips. I might not be able to move a limb, but perhaps I could twitch a finger. The frustration of sending a command to my body and getting no response was maddening. It was like shouting into a void. But I knew patience, perseverance, and consistent discipline were my only hope for progress.

As I battled my physical incapacitation, rumors circulated about an F-18 pilot with the call sign Shaka. His story became my beacon of hope. Shaka had experienced a similar high-speed ejection while undergoing the grueling TOPGUN course in Fallon, Nevada. Miraculously, he survived, but his body was left shattered like mine. However, he fought back into the cockpit through sheer grit, determination, and hard work, eventually becoming a TOPGUN instructor and later a commanding officer of a fighter squadron.

His story resonated deeply with me. If Shaka could overcome such insurmountable odds and return to the cockpit, maybe I could too. His journey, his victory, became the spark that ignited my fighting spirit, fanning the flames of my determination to recover.

At this pivotal moment, I made a crucial decision to stoke the tiny ember of hope ignited by Shaka's story. Instead of feeding the crushing negative emotions, I chose to visualize myself back in the cockpit of the Super Hornet. What if it was possible to return to the cockpit? What would it feel like to do so? How good it would feel to prove the pessimist wrong! As I stoked this positive mental image, the tiny ember of hope started to grow.

The ICU room was like a plexiglass fishbowl, filled with the constant beeping and humming of various medical monitors and equipment. Privacy was a luxury I didn't have, with medical staff constantly coming and going. An irritated patient in the neighboring room shouted at the nurses regardless of the hour. Despite the painkillers, my body began to throb with deep discomfort under the hot, sticky plastic wrap that covered my extremities. Sleep wouldn't come naturally initially, so the doctors put me in a medicated sleep-like state with an IV cocktail of synthetic opiates, far more potent than morphine.

One evening, while listening to Kid Cudi's album *Man on the Moon*, I had an almost transcendental experience after a hefty dose of synthetic joy. It felt like liquid bliss, slowly permeating through my veins. The music was visible, vibrant, and full spectrum, flowing into my shattered psyche. The sheer ecstasy I experienced carried me off into a serene dreamscape.

The morning arrived, bringing with it the dissipation of the drug-induced ecstasy. I woke up, my body smeared in my own waste, the harsh stench of hospital disinfectant mingling unpleasantly with the warmth of feces. The young and nonchalant corpsmen didn't bat an eye at cleaning me. I felt embarrassed, but he reassured me that this was part of his job. The upbeat young sailor had enlisted with aspirations of being a special operations combat medic, applying tourniquets under gunfire. Instead, he found himself wiping away the excrement from some baby-faced officer's pasty backside in a dilapidated navy training hospital, all while being hassled by overworked and underpaid nurses.

After weeks in the ICU fishbowl, I regained enough strength to shift around in bed. One morning, I miraculously managed to sit up. During her rounds, the nurse was startled to find me upright. My arms and legs remained unresponsive, but it was progress.

Removing the plastic wrap, stitches, and staples from my limbs was a welcome relief. My skin could breathe and be bathed for the first time in weeks. That first hot shower was almost as sublime as the Dilaudid.

I was eventually stable enough for transport to the Hunter Holmes McGuire Polytrauma Rehabilitation Center, a Department of Veterans Affairs hospital in Richmond, Virginia. The facility had just undergone a renovation, and the doctors assured me it was the best option in the surrounding area. Eager to kick-start my rehabilitation and escape Naval Hospital Portsmouth, I looked forward to the transfer.

*   *   *

Once admitted to the polytrauma center, my days were filled with various therapeutic activities: speech therapy, vision therapy, occupational therapy, physical therapy, kinesiotherapy, and recreational therapy. The facility had recently been refurbished, and it showed. Each room came equipped with a flat-screen TV and a high-tech adjustable bed. The freshly painted walls were adorned with pleasant artwork, and most staff seemed enthusiastic about their work. Although confined to a wheelchair, reliant on Tiffany for mobility, and suffering impaired cognitive functioning, I participated actively and cooperatively in my therapy sessions.

The VA polytrauma center was filled with service members grappling with various complex injuries. Many suffered IED attacks, explosions, and gunshot wounds, presenting with missing or surgically salvaged limbs. There was a navy explosives specialist (EOD) from the SEAL teams, Jake, who miraculously survived a skydiving mishap resulting in a high-speed impact that severely damaged his legs, pelvis, and internal organs.

An eighteen-year-old sailor lay in a vegetative state, his family squabbling over the lump sum insurance payment following a motorcycle accident with a distracted driver. Another young army infantryman was relearning to walk after being struck by a rocket-propelled grenade. At twenty-eight, I was among the oldest patients in the unit. These were just kids, their lives irrevocably altered by war.

As for the food, I had thought the fare at the Portsmouth Naval Hospital was subpar, but the meals served at the VA Polytrauma Center were truly deplorable. At least Portsmouth had a food court. Prepared by the lowest bidder in Hampton Roads, Virginia, the highly processed VA food was loaded into metal containers and transported to Richmond, an hour away. By the time the food trays were retrieved from their crates, they had formed a dry crust from the prolonged heating. Some patients were stuck on low-sodium, low-fat diets, which only exacerbated the tasteless nature of the food. My only consolation was being allowed hot sauce.

One meal I dubbed "the Holiday Feast," better than many served during my stay, featured near-rancid sliced turkey, slimy to the touch. The mashed potatoes were obviously from a box, with dry, powdery chunks of dehydrated starch still visible throughout the pale mass. The gravy on top looked like it had been plopped from a can of dog food, the can rings imprinted in the brown, gelatinous goop. To complete the festive spirit of the culinary delight was a white, generic jelly packet labeled "cranberry," which contained purple gelatin made from high fructose corn syrup and artificial coloring.

Despite all the funds poured into maintaining the optics of superior health care, it was pretty discouraging to witness the gross neglect of one of the most vital aspects of recovery: nutrition. Even though the hospital staff understood the abysmal quality of the food, they were handcuffed by an unyielding, bureaucratic system. The dietitian was merely adhering to the policies they were bound to follow. Despite her obsessive control issues, at least Tiffany brought me real food. However, most patients had no choice but to consume the nutrient-deprived gruel served to them daily. The lack of crucial nutrients undoubtedly stifled their recoveries.

Occasionally, the Wounded Warrior Project would treat us to freshly baked pizza. The pleasant aroma wafting through the sterile hallways concealed the constant stink of disinfectant. Pizza deliveries were accompanied by veterans of past wars, who would share their experiences with the VA from decades prior. One veteran, a former sniper in Vietnam, had been separated from his team after being shot multiple times. He told a harrowing tale of his escape, crawling through hostile jungle terrain, avoiding capture, and surviving until he was found by friendly forces days later. He painted a grim picture of the VA at that time: packing a dozen men in a room the size of my private one, many left groaning in pain, covered in their shit and crusted blood, with barely a daily nurse visit. Many became dependent on morphine and then discharged onto the streets. Their wheelchairs, crippling addictions, and nightmares were their only possessions. Despite being drafted into a war he hadn't chosen, critically injured, and battling years of addiction to opiates while living on the street, this man still maintained a strikingly positive outlook and proudly identified as an American veteran.

One particular ward at the polytrauma center was primarily occupied by combat veterans with permanent spinal injuries.

Despite their grim prognosis, with little to no hope of ever regaining the use of their arms or legs, their spirits were high. These individuals—former army infantrymen, marines, and Special Forces operators—maintained their indomitable attitudes. Their positive mindsets were infectious as they wheelied their wheelchairs around the hospital, determined to make the best of their circumstances.

Due to shooting nerve pain, I was on an ever-expanding list of pain medications and drugs to counteract the numerous side effects. My cocktail of pharmaceuticals included oxycodone, oxycontin, gabapentin, tramadol, trazodone, and amitriptyline, among others. Despite my regular intake of a fiber supplement, my bowel movements came to a standstill.

Despite all the painkillers, I was experiencing severe nerve pain in my left leg and foot randomly. This pain disrupted my sleep and marred my waking hours. Sometimes, it felt like my toes were being crushed with pliers; other times, it was as though a car battery had been hooked up to my leg and foot, sending electric shocks that made me wince in agony. On the worst days, it felt like my leg was on fire or a combination of all the above. None of the pain medications managed to halt the suffering, but they indeed shot me higher than a CCP weather balloon sailing over the Montana skyline.

Pharmaceutical companies were crafty with their trials, employing gorgeous, charismatic female representatives to entice injured service members into signing up for experimental medical treatments. These representatives were dressed between business casual and high-end escort, effectively getting trial volunteers. After overhearing a grim discussion among the staff about a disastrous trial that had backfired on the spinal unit, I abstained from participating.

Paralyzed patients suffering from nerve pain had experimental medication injected into their spinal fluid, only for it to inflict them with permanent, excruciating pain. Supposedly, the medication, cryogenically stored in containers unfit for liquid nitrogen, had been contaminated. The patients in this trial reportedly begged to be put out of their misery, their screams of pain only silenced when they were placed into induced comas. Unbeknownst to the public, wounded servicemembers are used as lab rats by the pharmaceutical industry.

My sleep was disrupted and rarely restful. I was heavily medicated into a state of unconsciousness resembling sleep. Once knocked out, I would frequently be woken up to take more medications and check my vitals. It felt like the doctors were more proficient in prescribing drugs than understanding the fundamentals of health, such as the importance of restful sleep and nutrition. As my tolerance to the medications grew, so did the prescribed doses.

One day, a man with long hair, kind eyes, and a small leather bag entered my room like he wasn't supposed to be there. He briefly explained a treatment called prolotherapy, where he would inject small amounts of glucose into my skin around areas of nerve pain. This process required my consent, unlike the barrage of pharmaceuticals I was on. He spent less than ten minutes injecting my leg with glucose, which left it looking like it was covered in swollen mosquito bites. The relentless nerve pain dissipated as he worked his way up my leg. Most of my leg's random shooting nerve pain was gone when he was done. Even to this day, the nerve pain in my leg has never returned with the same intensity. All it took was a hippy doctor with some sugar water.

Over time, I fell into a routine and noticed slight improvements. My right arm remained paralyzed, but I learned to use my nondominant hand. Due to the median nerve damage, only my pinky and ring finger functioned, leaving half of my hand numb and limp. With those two fingers and a barely functioning left bicep, I relearned how to brush my teeth and eat. The skill of wiping my ass still eluded me. However, the regained function in my left hand enabled me to operate an electric wheelchair, giving me a newfound sense of liberation after months of dependency.

Despite the significant reduction in pain from the prolotherapy, the medical team increased my dose of gabapentin to a whopping 2,400 milligrams a day. They justified this by saying gabapentin was much safer than the opioids I took simultaneously. Yet I continued the same dose of opioids once I ramped up on gabapentin. The medical clergy-folk, indoctrinated as pharmaceutical drug pushers, insisted that it was essential to maintain a consistent medication regimen, warning that reducing the dosage could lead to intractable pain. Their fear tactics, a regurgitation of what they had been taught from the gospel of medical journals saturated with pharmaceutical propaganda, were challenging to combat with my lack of knowledge at the time.

On rare occasions, the recreational therapist arranged short bus adventures. Wheelchair-bound vets had the opportunity to journey into town, savoring a meal that didn't remind us of reheated soggy cardboard with a side of dumpster bisque.

As I entered the eatery on my first outing since the crash, the divine scent of freshly cooked chow hit me, a smell I had never appreciated more. The sensory delight seemed to stimulate my dormant bowels, which, thanks to the high dosage of painkillers, had been plugging up my pipes tighter than Scrooge McDuck's vault.

Tiffany wheeled me into the restroom and plopped me onto the toilet seat like she was mounting a 180-pound toddler onto a tricycle. At the "Fight's on," there was a fleeting sense of relief as I finally managed to initiate a bowel movement. However, it quickly became apparent that this adversary wasn't coming out without a brawl. The straining turned into screams as something large and unyielding ripped its way out like the creature from *Alien*. My howls echoed in the restaurant. The music volume increased as the staff attempted to drown out my screams of agony, but the sound of a man pitted against his insides was not one easily subdued.

The marathon battle eventually ended victoriously with a large mass, the size and shape of an oversized frag grenade, finally being jettisoned. I was half expecting a Purple Heart as I tranquility admired the payload. Awkwardly leaving the un-flushable collateral damage behind, I wheeled from the warzone to notice that staff and guests had become oddly interested in their shoes. Fortunately, no one had notified local law enforce-ment. Stomach Winchester, I enjoyed a freshly cooked meal despite my permanently traumatized sphincter.

*   *   *

Weeks crept into months of therapy sessions and hard work. One day, to my amazement, I found myself wiggling the fingers of my right hand. Despite the doc's grim prognosis insisting I would never use my right arm again, I was making tangible progress. Did they somehow know telling me I couldn't do something would only motivate me more?

Within a few days, I was able to scribble my name. The let-ters were clumsy and childlike, but it was forward motion. Not long after, I regained enough control to wipe my ass unassisted. Victory!

CHAPTER 19

Tiffany, like the manipulative nurse Annie Wilkes from Stephen King's *Misery*, had been a constant presence since I awoke from my coma. She meticulously detailed all she had done for me while I was unconscious, crafting an image of herself as indispensable. At first, I appreciated her support, grateful for her seemingly unwavering dedication. But beneath the surface, she was weaving a web of lies, carefully constructing an alternate reality designed to entangle me and push away those who truly cared.

With my cognitive abilities severely diminished from my brain injury, I became the perfect target for her manipulation. Tiffany planted seeds of doubt about everyone around me, starting with my mother. She spun stories about my mother's supposed incompetence, claiming she was losing essential documents, mismanaging my care, and causing unnecessary problems with the staff. These were complete fabrications, but in my foggy, dazed state—fueled by brain trauma and heavy medications—I went along with her. My mother was desperately trying to protect me from Tiffany's growing influence. My fear of Tiffany's threats to make false accusations about me abusing her and her son still lingered in the back of my mind, further complicating the situation. The manipulation worked. I tearfully asked my heartbroken mother to return home. Her only son had been ripped from her grasp.

My mother's departure marked the point of no return. Tiffany had successfully isolated me from my family. Tears streamed down my mother's face as she left, powerless to reach me through the haze of lies and threats Tiffany had woven around me. And with my family pushed aside, Tiffany's grip tightened. She made sure I believed my squadron mates were unreliable, too, convincing me that they had abandoned me during my time of need. They had been trying to stay involved, but Tiffany had expertly kept them at bay. I was unaware the missed calls from concerned squadron mates were piling up on my phone.

It was all part of her plan—an intricate, calculated effort to alienate everyone who might challenge her authority. The cocktail of brain injury, painkillers, and cowardice left me pliable, and she seized that moment to assert total control. She began to steer the conversation toward marriage, dangling the idea of "taking care of me" and the benefits she might receive as my caregiver. Behind her sweet promises, I could sense an undercurrent of calculation. She wasn't doing this out of love; she was angling for something far more self-serving.

Tiffany's influence deepened with time at the polytrauma center. She continued to control the narrative, manipulating my perception of reality and isolating me further. She had taken control of my phone, tablet, and social media accounts. She even went as far as posting on social media that we were married—without my knowledge or consent. It was another step in her strategy to tighten her hold on me. Receiving the news that her son had spontaneously married a destructive woman, my mother was devastated. She mailed me a burner phone, hoping to communicate, but Tiffany quickly intercepted it and hid it. Still lacking the use of my hands, I couldn't have used it without help. I was completely reliant on her.

Looking back, I can see how insidious her manipulation was. I had been physically and mentally immobilized, trapped in a version of reality that Tiffany had crafted for her benefit. I was a prisoner of her deceit and threats, cut off from my family, my friends, and even my judgment, as she slowly built a world where only she held the keys.

As I struggled to regain my faculties at the polytrauma center, an investigation into my accident unfolded. My memory was clouded, and my cognition was stunted. Regardless, I was pressed for every detail of the incident I could recall. From what I had eaten in the days leading up to the accident to the state of my relationship with Tiffany, everything was under scrutiny. I had been at the controls of an 89-million-dollar aircraft that was now destroyed. The pressure of the investigation was crushing. Had this all been my fault? And what would the consequences be if it had been?

One morning, as Tiffany assisted me in preparing for my therapy session, a man of commanding presence strode unannounced into my room. Dressed in a flight suit decorated with chaplain insignia, his demeanor was far from a soothing man of God. Cursory questions about my religious beliefs quickly pivoted to probing inquiries about my relationship with Tiffany, who was attentively observing the interrogation. My responses were guarded. There was something about this stranger that made me uneasy. I couldn't shake off the thought that he might be from the Naval Criminal Investigative Service (NCIS) under the guise of a chaplain. My lack of sleep, traumatic brain injury, and medication cocktail occasionally bred paranoia. When his line of questioning petered out, he made an abrupt exit. The stress of my life unraveling was crushing, so I focused on my recovery, swallowed down the negative emotions, and buried them deep within me.

Once strong enough to maneuver a non-powered wheel-chair over short distances, I gained a new level of freedom. I could get into a regular vehicle and venture out to lunch without requiring a ride on the recreational therapy short bus. During one such outing with Tiffany, I noticed she had my phone with a missed call from Fisty. Until that point, I had been too weak to use my phone. Tiffany had been "keeping an eye on it" for me. Seeing an opportunity, I made a move. Despite the misleading fabrications Tiffany had been feeding me about my squadron mate's dubious loyalty, I wanted to call Fisty back. The four-hour round trip between Virginia Beach and Richmond made it impractical for guys to visit often. Tiffany responded aggressively as I reached my shaky arm for the phone. She swerved into the center median of the busy four-lane highway, bringing the Jeep to an abrupt stop.

Swiftly, she snatched the phone from my weak grip and berated me, "No one gives a fuck about you except me!" Enraged, she exited the 4x4, pulled my wheelchair from the trunk, and hastily shoved me into it amidst the rushing traffic. "If your squadron cares so much about you, they can come to pick you up!" she screamed, slamming the passenger door shut. Helplessly, I watched her drive off in *my* Grand Cherokee. I was stranded in the middle of a bustling city street, broken.

With my arms still weak, I didn't make it far. I sat there, stuck, feeling utterly powerless. Tiffany's words echoed in my mind, amplifying my feelings of abandonment, isolation, and hopelessness. As I began to look for a silver lining—freedom from her constant threats and emotional manipulation—I saw my Grand Cherokee returning. Tiffany came back and offered another of her practiced apologies. She wrestled me back into the car, and we continued our outing. The freshly cooked restaurant food, at least, had been enjoyable.

CHAPTER 20

After several more weeks of dedicated rehabilitation, I regained more mobility using a walker. I moved about slowly, teetering and shuffling, reminiscent of a little old lady, but each small victory kept me motivated. I continued to immerse myself in my recovery as a distraction from the precarious situation in which I found myself. After three months of strenuous efforts, I was finally cleared to return to Virginia Beach, where I would continue my treatment as an outpatient at Naval Hospital Portsmouth.

Despite being grateful to the therapists and staff who had helped me during my stay, I certainly wouldn't miss the VA. Relieved to be free from the restrictive, bureaucratic policies, the disgusting hospital slop, the late-night disruptions for check-ups, and the pervasive smell of disinfectant, I watched as the VA hospital receded in the rearview mirror, fervently hoping that I would never have to return.

In Virginia Beach, calls for continuing the Field Naval Aviator Evaluation Board, or FNAEB, became louder. An FNAEB investigation is launched whenever a Class A mishap—a significant incident resulting in severe injury or destruction to over 1 million dollars of equipment—occurs. The F/A-18E Super Hornet, now in countless fragments, drifting in the abyss of the Atlantic, was valued at 89 million dollars in 2014. I continued to grapple with the idea that I might be responsible for such a massive loss.

The goal of the investigation was to learn what exactly happened to help prevent the same mishap from unfolding again. Lessons learned in blood could become valuable case studies and lead to improved practices. The FNAEB could also result in serious disciplinary action. It hung over me like a warhead dangling by a thread.

Some of my squadron mates, trying to lighten the situation, jokingly suggested that I owed each American taxpayer a gumball after they did the math. Despite their much-appreciated humor, I found myself nervously chewing my numb fingernails until they bled as the stress escalated.

Suffering from allodynia, which made my swollen feet extraordinarily sensitive to touch, I squeezed into a fresh pair of standard-issue brown leather steel-toe flight boots, grimacing with each movement. Incapable of driving, I required a ride from Tiffany, whose care I still relied on despite the continued abuse. On base, I limped through the building with my walker, aiming for a dimly lit room on the second floor of the NAS Oceana F/A-18 simulator building. This was where the initial board would conduct the preliminary FNAEB interviews.

During this initial investigation phase, a group of aviators from my air wing, CAG-7, interviewed me and several other squadron members. Fortunately, each of my fellow squadron mates testified that I was an above-average pilot for my experience level and well-liked within the squadron.

The aircraft data recorder, the "black box," had been recovered from the ejection seat. This allowed the flight to be reviewed in detail. The recording and interviews helped conclude that I executed a split-S maneuver at an airspeed above the TOP-GUN recommendation while distracted by the operation of my new JHMCS helmet. A maneuver that would usually require around five thousand feet of vertical space consumed more than twice that when the flight control computer (FCC) engaged what is known as the G-bucket to protect from potential over-stress at such high speed. The FCC was responding to a bomb code previously programmed into the aircraft mission computer that I was unaware of. The Super Hornet thought there were heavy bombs on the wings that were not there.

This was the vertical equivalent of going around a sharp corner in a sports car only to have the steering wheel unexpectedly ease and become unresponsive at the apex of the turn. Instead of skidding off the road, I was trapped in an out-of-control dive at the worst possible moment.

Unlike most modern fighter aircraft, the FCC's inability to communicate with the ground proximity warning system (GPWS) significantly restricted the jet's turning ability at the worst possible moment. This led to the collision with the ocean. I could have potentially overridden the G-limiter by depressing the paddle switch on the base of the control stick, but I didn't recognize the complex situation in the few seconds I had to react.

My flight lead had heroically saved my life with his quick thinking during the rescue effort but was criticized for setting up our final fight outside the TOPGUN standard parameters. The higher-than-recommended starting airspeed and lower altitude created a dangerous situation that should have been avoided at my experience level. Although several contributing factors were beyond my control, my split-second error was a heavy burden.

Above all else, pressure was mounting to end my destructive relationship with Tiffany. My inability to deal with the deteriorating fling was considered a contributing human factor in the mishap.

To see how others would react in the same situation, several VFA-143 pilots were put into the simulator. They were provided with no prior knowledge of what happened in my case to avoid skewing the results. They were instructed to go nose-low at the high-speed merge, just like I had. Every pilot, even the most experienced, opted to eject, not having the reaction time to hit the paddle switch when the G-limiter was insidiously activated. While my decision to go nose-low should have been avoided, at least my decision to eject was validated.

After combing through my detailed aviation training records, the board considered nearly every mistake I made over almost four years of military flying. The grueling scrutiny was stifling. When the investigators asked me if I routinely made poor decisions and if I deserved to be a pilot, I choked back tears. It felt as though my impostor syndrome had been right all along. *Did I belong here?* My self-hatred boiled me alive from within. After a long pause, I affirmed that being a pilot had been my passion since childhood. Despite being far from a rockstar aviator, I desired to return to the cockpit to ride the beast that bucked me into the sound barrier. Consternation crowded the room.

The initial board concluded that I initiated a nose-low maneuver at an airspeed higher than recommended by TOP-GUN. However, several more experienced pilots had fallen into the same trap. The G-bucket of the Super Hornet had been a contributing factor in numerous past mishaps and close calls. In exchange for protection from a perceived minor overstress from a nonexistent loadout, the jet's FCC overrode my control inputs, leading to a catastrophic collision. The board also determined that with the tactical hard deck in place due to budget cuts, pilots were barely getting enough flight time to remain current, let alone proficient. As a rookie F/A-18 pilot, this was especially detrimental.

All factors considered, the preliminary board recommended an A2, which would allow me to keep my wings. The slim chance to return to flying was a sip of relief. However, the final, formal segment of the FNAEB loomed: a hearing before a larger panel of experienced aviators and an admiral who would make the final decision. I anxiously awaited their verdict, channeling my nervous energy into my recovery.

CHAPTER 21

In their human factors analysis, investigators identified my deteriorating relationship with Tiffany as a contributing factor to the mishap. The pressure to end the relationship was escalating. Despite my growing resentment toward her oppressive control and cunning, manipulative tactics, the fear of her threatening accusations still haunted me. I sought an escape without provoking her wrath, but I was effectively imprisoned; she had taken possession of my phone, wallet, and vehicle. Furthermore, my need for a caregiver kept me bound to her residence, leaving me captive. I attempted a prison break in my underwear but couldn't even make it down the stairs unassisted.

During my extensive inpatient tenure, Tiffany assumed the reins of my personal life. She dominated my phone, finances, car, and social media presence. Dictating the minutiae from my visitors to my breakfast menu, she orchestrated a regime of stringent control. With calculated precision, she alienated my closest confidants, including my mother and squadron mates, monitoring my every breath. Partly, my reluctance to seek help from my squadron mates sprung from embarrassment and cowardice, feeling inadequate to handle the machinations of a petite brunette single-handedly. However, her manipulative charade had run its course, and my squadron mates embarked on a mission to free me.

Fisty, the embodiment of heroism, drove to my rescue in his movie-quality 1994 *Jurassic Park*-themed Jeep Wrangler. The sound of the engine roaring to life outside the house was my first glimmer of hope. I could hear Tiffany's frantic footsteps as she rushed to the door, her voice cracking with desperation as she pleaded something like, "Please, don't leave me! We can work this out!"

Tom "Fisty" Flynn. The man. The legend.

Ignoring the pang of guilt that twisted in my chest, I hastened to pack a duffle bag with essential belongings. My weak, nerve-damaged hands trembled as I stuffed clothes and personal items into the bag, the urgency of the moment making every second feel like an eternity. Still unable to navigate a set of stairs unaided, I felt a surge of panic. How was I going to get out of here?

Just then, Fisty burst through the door, his face set with determination. The look in his eyes boomed, "Let's get you the fuck out of here." He grabbed my small duffle of belongings and, with the strength of his sturdy frame, helped me down the stairwell.

As we made our way to the Jeep, Tiffany's cries grew louder, more desperate. "Don't leave me! You can't do this!" she screamed, tears streaming down her desperate face. But I knew I had to go. Her manipulative hold on me had to end.

Fisty helped me into the passenger seat, quickly throwing my walker and duffle into the back seat. As we sped away, the sound of her cries diminishing in the distance, it felt like evading a pursuing T-Rex. The metaphor was fitting, given the *Jurassic Park*-themed Jeep, but it also captured the sheer terror and relief of the moment. My heart pounded in my chest, a mix of fear and exhilaration.

Looking dapper with Fisty the year following my release from the hospital.

My new sanctuary was to be with Fisty and another close ally from flight school, Vinny. The drive to their place was a blur of emotions. I glanced back at the house one last time, feeling a strange mix of sorrow and liberation. At last, I was free from the seductive succubus.

As we pulled into the driveway of Fisty's peaceful wooded home, I felt a weight lift off my shoulders. The nightmare was over. I was surrounded by friends who genuinely cared about me and who had risked their own safety to rescue me from a toxic situation. I felt a much-needed surge of hope.

Fisty helped me inside, and Vinny greeted me with a warm smile and a firm handshake. "Welcome home, Big Guy," he beamed, and I knew he meant it.

The road to recovery would be long and challenging, but I was no longer alone. With the support of my friends, I could begin to rebuild my life, free from Tiffany's oppressive control. The future was uncertain, but it was mine to shape, and that was a freedom worth fighting for.

CHAPTER 22

Once I had found some stability living with Fisty and Vinny, I resumed my outpatient therapies at Portsmouth Naval Hospital. My squadron mates took turns braving the chaotic traffic on Highway 264 to transport me to my endless schedule of medical appointments.

Soon, a new issue arose: My left knee was causing shooting pain whenever fully extended. X-rays revealed that the titanium rod in my left tibia was protruding into the knee joint when the leg was locked straight. Another surgery was necessary to rectify the complication. Yet again, disaster loomed.

I arrived at Naval Hospital Portsmouth well before sunrise on the morning of what was to be my thirteenth surgical procedure following the ejection. After changing into a hospital gown, a disgruntled nurse insisted on painfully jabbing the IV port into a tiny blood vessel in my pinky finger despite several more suitable veins. Any of them, really! The port placement was uncomfortable and highly unusual, but the anesthesia soon quelled the discomfort as I drifted asleep.

I gradually regained consciousness after the surgery, finding myself in a wheelchair positioned awkwardly by the entrance of the hospital lobby. My wispy hospital gown offered little to no privacy, leaving my bare ass exposed to the bustling hospital environment. Usually, patients are monitored in a recovery room post-surgery. Instead, I was left alone, drowsily nodding in and out of consciousness with the opening and closing of the automatic exit doors. Eventually, a nurse found me and questioned my peculiar location. Unable to give her a coherent answer, she kindly wheeled me into a shared room to stay overnight.

My roommate, a gentleman hidden behind a privacy curtain, remained faceless throughout our stay. Our room was attended by a young and visibly nervous corpsman, fresh out of training and lost in the grand scheme of hospital protocols. He mumbled what sounded like a checklist as he struggled with my patient assessment. His lack of experience was only matched by a butter bar nurse who failed to place a new IV port in my forearm correctly. To help me rehydrate, he hooked me up to an IV bag of saline solution, but the misplaced port caused fluid to pool under my skin, swelling like a fleshy water balloon.

As time passed, I repeatedly raised my concerns to the corpsman, explaining that the IV appeared to be placed subcutaneously. He dismissed my concerns with a nervous glance and little understanding of the situation.

Gradually, as the anesthesia wore off, I began feeling raw pain from my surgical wounds. It was uncomfortable but bearable. However, I soon started to feel overwhelmingly nauseous and weak. My dehydration worsened due to the misplaced IV, and I started experiencing withdrawal symptoms from the plethora of pain medications I had grown dependent on in the preceding months. My regular doses were long overdue. There was a pharmacy in the building, but with this medical team, it might as well have been in Syria. My body began trembling as I alternated between pouring sweat and uncontrollable chills.

Still oblivious to my worsening condition, the bumbling corpsman returned with a small plastic urinal and requested that I piss on demand. With my dehydration worsening by the minute, the mere thought of this inconsiderate request irritated me, only to exacerbate my misery further. I was writhing in deep pain, moaning in agony with sporadic yells as the throbbing discomfort spiked. While catching my breath between worsening waves of severe pain, I apologized to my unseen roommate for the disturbance. He had become an involuntary audience to the suffering of someone on the verge of demise.

The corpsman insisted that to be discharged, I had to prove my mobility by walking to the room at the end of the hall, roughly a two-hundred-foot odyssey. I would do anything to get the fuck out of this hellhole. Gritting my teeth against the intense pain, I clung to my walker and took that first excruciating step on my freshly operated leg, dysfunctional IV in tow. Each step was a trial, marked by the unbearable crunch of bone as the new titanium rod and screws settled into place. After what felt like grinding through an Ironman triathlon on a broken leg without hydration, I stumbled into a room at the end of the hall, exhausted. The medical staff inside watched in disbelief as I collapsed onto the white tile floor, dry heaving while gasping for air. They were courteous enough to bring me a trash can, at least.

Hours of unrelenting pain crept by. The combination of withdrawal symptoms, post-surgery pain, and severe dehydration continued to tear me apart. I was slowly dying in that sweat-drenched bed in the most miserable pain of my life. The irony of the situation was not lost on me: a novice pilot injured partly due to his inexperience was now in the hands of inexperienced medical staff. The thought crossed my mind that maybe I deserved this.

With great effort, a tablespoon's worth of dark brown urine oozed into the handheld urinal, finally convincing the startled corpsman and nurse of the issue with the IV. It was about time they took me seriously.

It was well past the last call when the doc wheeled in a batch of long overdue IV pain medication. Finally, a drop of relief, though the pain raged on like wildfire, scorching my internals alive. I anxiously awaited the sound of the patient-controlled medicine (PCM) device clicking, signaling that another metered dose of liquid bliss was available at the push of a button. The minutes dragged by, begging to hear "click." Each surge of Dilaudid was merely a bucket of water to the inferno within, but at least it was something.

My regular medications finally arrived by midday, and the miserable withdrawal symptoms slowly eased. KC, another friend and fellow aviator, showed up to take me home. The discharge process dragged on until the late afternoon. As KC helped me depart, I noticed a poster on an easel proudly displaying the hospital's outstanding patient satisfaction over the past year. The irony was palpable.

CHAPTER 23

I felt as though my life was in ruins. I had gone from having my dream job to being a drug-addicted, ill, and depressed wreck with a bleak future. The ramifications of that split-second decision haunted me relentlessly. My career, relationship, physical health, and mental state were all in shambles.

One sunny afternoon, as I sat alone poolside at Fisty and Vinny's place, my scarred, swollen, pasty body soaking up the much-needed sun, I took a generous swig of whiskey to wash down a handful of oxycodone. Had Tiffany not hoarded it, along with most of my possessions, I would have opened the bottle Mr. Stock, my college professor, had gifted me before I left for OCS. As the artificial relief set in, every worry and concern I had seemed to melt away. I sank deeper into the patio chair, immersing myself in a chemically induced euphoria.

*   *   *

After what felt like an eternity of treading water in the sea of uncertainty, I finally received a date for my formal FNAEB. Dressed in my summer white uniform's crisp, clean lines, I navigated to Naval Air Station Norfolk. Before meeting with the admiral, I faced a formidable audience of a dozen experienced aviators, each representing a unique sector of the naval aviation community. Their inquiries about my mishap were respectfully posed. I met their queries head-on, confessing candidly that I had erred in the heat of a split-second decision. The assembled aviators understood that my misstep was magnified by a control feature that had tripped up seasoned pilots. Luckily, the officers holding my fate in their hands were all naval aviators. They recognized the inherent risks and inevitable mishaps of pushing these high-power aircraft to their limits. No veteran pilot is without a tale of a close call. Some had even weathered mishaps of their own. The preliminary meeting appeared to unfold favorably.

I was ushered out as the board retreated behind closed doors to deliberate my case. It wasn't long before I was called back into the shark tank. I was perched at the end of the imposing hardwood table, flanked on either side by the seasoned aviators. With the entrance of the admiral, we rose in unison from our seats. His calm directive for us to sit was followed by taking his place at the helm of the table. An uncomfortable hush filled the room, lingering longer than one would like.

Breaking the silence, the admiral's gaze met mine down the length of the table. "Lieutenant Gill, are you fearless?" he asked bluntly.

I bowed my head for a moment, mulling over my response. The phrase etched onto the Pukin' Dogs' crest is *Sans reproche*, meaning "without fear." I suspect he wanted to confirm if I was a madman. He likely already knew.

Whether it was the residual effect of my medication or some divine intervention, I found myself boldly stating as I raised my gaze to meet the admiral's, "Sir, I can't recall every detail from the ejection, but I am certain what little cushion there was on the ejection seat was puckered up inside me real tight."

His face remained impassive, his eyes never leaving mine. The air sucked out of the room. Without uttering a word, he rose from his seat. We mirrored his action as he made his swift exit from the room. My heart was pounding wildly.

Unsettled, I was led out of the boardroom and into the office of one of the high-ranking officers from the board. As I sat, he offered me a Life Savers mint from a glass jar on his hardwood desk. As I popped the mint into my mouth, I was still in the dark about what had just transpired. His outstretched hand and warm smile shattered my confusion. His congratulations confirmed that I would retain my wings. If I could recover fully, I'd be given another shot at flying Super Hornets.

A profound wave of relief swept over me; it felt like I could finally draw a full breath again. Even though the FNAEB investigation was closed, I still had to overcome the recovery hurdle, wean off all medications, and secure a stack of medical waivers for a catalog of injuries. A few more miracles wouldn't hurt.

CHAPTER 24

The recovery journey continued a seemingly endless parade of medical appointments, therapy sessions, and workouts. During my recovery, I was assigned to the operations department of Strike Fighter Wing Atlantic, CSFWL. The place was a common holding area for aviators wrestling with health issues or other struggles that kept them out of the cockpit; we fondly referred to it as "the Land of Misfit Toys."

Being a physical therapist herself, Amanda "Aunt Smuggs" Johnson, the wife of a squadron mate, volunteered her time to work with me. Her approach freed me from the sterile white boredom of clinical therapy into the raw grit of no-rules beat-down recovery. I came hobbling in with my cane on day one, only to have her snatch it and toss it aside. "I don't want to catch you using that bullshit again," she half-joked. "Patients' Tears" was proudly written on her water bottle. She was the sharp-edged but warmhearted guide I needed.

With a wealth of experience under her belt and a dark sense of humor in her toolkit, Amanda was an ace. Her work at the physical therapy clinic had grown tedious due to the whining patients seeking the easy way out. I was her breath of fresh air, a patient willing to give everything to the grueling recovery process. She gave me a workout, and I'd attack it with all my strength. Months rolled by, and I morphed from a staggering walker to a runner, donning a weighted vest and conquering laps around the base track. Thanks to Aunt Smugg's hard-charging modalities, I was recovering rapidly.

When not immersed in therapy, I gradually took on various responsibilities at the wing. Admittedly, sitting glued to a computer screen bathed in harsh fluorescent light wasn't my preferred activity, but I diligently applied myself to the tasks whenever I wasn't attending medical appointments. Thankfully, my generous boss allowed me to prioritize my therapy and self-imposed brutal workout sessions.

Against the pain management clinic's counsel, I started weaning myself off my medications. One by one, I gradually began to step away from a cocktail of pain meds, including amitriptyline, tramadol, and trazodone. Slowly but surely, I reduced each dosage, tuning in closely to my body's response. When withdrawal symptoms became too brutal, I'd dial the dose back up slightly before lowering it further.

My next challenge was to curb my intake of oxycodone and oxycontin. Though I anticipated this would be the most challenging part, within a month, I was free from their grip.

The final hurdle was breaking free from the daily 2,400 milligrams of gabapentin. This drug was initially marketed as a safe, nonaddictive alternative to opioids. Yet the scientific studies, manipulated and funded by pharmaceutical corporations, seemed dubious at best.

For a deeper dive into the corruption lurking behind these so-called gold-standard, peer-reviewed, double-blind placebo clinical trials that physicians trust like gospel, I highly recommend *Sickening: How Big Pharma Broke American Health Care and How We Can Repair It* by Dr. John Abramson. He illuminates how pharmaceutical companies can selectively cherry-pick data from these trials for submission to peer review. Instead of an entire trial undergoing peer review, the drug company submits only a selective analysis. As Dr. Abramson points out, these companies essentially referee their own games and have been found rigging the process on multiple occasions. Any fines incurred when caught are paltry compared to the profits from such practices. The makers of gabapentin lost a landmark lawsuit when it was discovered they had illegally marketed the drug for off-label use. However, the subsequent fine was a mere slap on the wrist—a tolerable cost of doing business—and the same practices continue today unabated.

Eliminating gabapentin from my system was a long, agonizing slog that spanned several months. I followed the same gradual reduction process as the other drugs. However, the symptoms of withdrawal—weakness, restlessness, cold sweats, and nausea—demanded a more gradual tapering. Daily bouts of lightheadedness, a scattered mind, and a perpetual inability to relax made the process much harder. Even as the weakness and nausea tried to bring me down, I managed to claw my way through to the other side, albeit with fingernails chewed down to their nubs.

Once I was finally free of all medications, my body and mind began to show marked improvement. My free time transitioned from exhaustion on the couch in front of the TV to lively dinners with friends. My dormant libido reawakened with vigor. I turned to the app Lumosity to help rebuild my brain. Astonishingly, my scores on these brain-training games improved exponentially within a few weeks of dropping the medications. Physically, I began to regain muscle tone and shed the extra weight I'd accumulated, and my bowels resumed their normal functions. Even my skin started to regain its healthy glow.

One lingering issue was the severed median nerve in my left forearm, which had robbed my index, middle finger, and thumb of their functionality. I reluctantly returned to Naval

Hospital Portsmouth, where I met with the experienced orthopedic surgeon, Dr. Christopher Hogan. Dr. Hogan's colossal hand dwarfed mine as we shook, his broad physique befitting a professional football player. His vibrant personality radiated a confidence that inspired trust. He shared that he had discovered a procedure born out of the vile medical experiments conducted by Nazi doctors during World War II. These monstrous methods had uncovered a way to split tendons and reconnect them to nonfunctioning body parts. Despite the stomach-churning history, this knowledge is now used for healing in the modern era, like the technology that rebuilt my skeleton.

Arriving early on the morning of the procedure, I met with the nurse anesthetist tasked with my sedation. With a grin, he promised to be my bartender for the day, his cocktail of choice being the sedative ketamine. A painless IV in my arm was all it took for me to drift into peaceful oblivion.

Dr. Hogan first tackled the issue of heterotopic ossification (HO), a condition that had caused an overgrowth of bone, binding my left radius and ulna together and preventing forearm rotation. Having dealt with the HO, he proceeded with the tendon-splitting procedure, attaching a split tendon from my wrist to my thumb and one from my middle finger to my index finger.

Emerging from the anesthetic haze felt like ascending from the bottom of a warm, shallow, rainbow-colored tropical reef. The world shimmered and flowed around me as though viewed through the crystal-clear waters of the Caribbean Sea. The joyful, positive feelings surpassed the usual groggy nausea from waking from a general anesthetic. It turns out ketamine is a potent psychedelic as well. The surgery had succeeded. And this time, there was no post-op recovery disaster to contend with.

CHAPTER 25

Fisty and Vinny would toss me onto their boat on their rare days off, steering me into a day of wake surfing with the crew. I was all but a toddler in the walking department, but their stoke wouldn't let me back down. Their camaraderie and ceaseless cheer were uplifting, guiding me out of the deep abyss I'd found myself in. My legs quivered as Fisty hit the throttle while my noodle arms battled with the tow rope. Yet the surge of positivity got me riding the wake, a grin painted on my face. *If I could surf behind a boat, maybe I could even handle a legit ocean swell.* I wondered if being held under a wave would reignite the terror I had experienced while trapped in the parachute, but excitement soon got the better of me.

My buddies extended an invitation for a surfing escapade to Duck, North Carolina, nestled in the Outer Banks. Slipping into the wet suit posed a considerable challenge, given my arms' residual weakness. Nonetheless, the sight of the towering, ten-to-twelve-foot glassy barrels sent a rush of adrenaline coursing through my veins. Choosing to body surf, I strapped on a pair of fins, forgoing the cumbersome surfboard my shoulders were still incapable of paddling. The waves in the Outer Banks are notoriously swift and fierce, demanding respect even from experienced surfers.

As a formidable swell loomed, I marshaled all my strength into a powerful kick, reveling in the wave's force sweeping me.

But within a split second, the wave's fury unleashed, hurling me into the unforgiving sandbar below. Disoriented and gasping for air, I wrestled against the undercurrents, striving to breach the water's surface. Before I could breathe, another powerful wave drove me back down. Fighting against the aquatic onslaught, I clawed back to the surface, gulping the life-giving air. Vinny and my new roommate Neal paddled up after the waves passed and quipped, "Dude, I thought you were dead . . . again!"

The experience was a potent cocktail of fear and exhilaration, a raw confrontation with the elements that left me feeling alive. I feared that perhaps being held under would trigger PTSD, but instead, it rebuilt my confidence.

*   *   *

In another daring outing, my close friend Spicoli roped me into downhill mountain biking at Bryce Bike Park. With his loyal canine companion, Ruff, we embarked on an adventurous pilgrimage to the scenic Blue Ridge Mountains of Northern Virginia. Trail riding was familiar territory for me, but the complex challenges of rugged downhill riding were a new beast altogether. Clad in body armor, knee pads, and a full-face helmet, I charged the trails, full-send, fueled by Spicoli's unwavering support.

Our adventure was interspersed with hair-raising moments, not the least of which was Spicoli's old RV gasping for life, threatening to conk out on the twisty, mountainous roads. At one unnerving point, like The Little Engine That Couldn't, we began to roll backward down a steep incline, teetering perilously close to a deep ravine. But thanks to Spicoli's quick reflexes, we narrowly escaped the jaws of catastrophe.

Navigating the rowdy downhill riding proved challenging, with my weakened left hand barely holding onto the front brake and my recuperating legs still learning to balance. Yet, against all odds, I survived the mountain bike adventure unscathed. These raw and thrilling experiences amid the wilderness transformed into a unique form of therapy, far surpassing any healing a sterile clinic could provide. Nature is medicine.

Spicoli's unwavering support and friendship motivated me to transcend my physical limitations. Once back in Virginia Beach, we seized any opportunity to hit the Oceanfront waves whenever a surfable swell appeared on the surf cams. Gradually, my shoulders grew stronger, and my precarious balance steadied. I experienced countless wipeouts and tumbles in the churning ocean, but, fueled by Spicoli's infectious enthusiasm, it was impossible not to paddle back into the surf for one more wave.

I was honored to be the best man for my brother Aaron "Spicoli" Thurber. Following him through the rugged mountains and pounding ocean swell helped me rebuild my broken body in ways that could not be accomplished in a clinical setting.

CHAPTER 26

Meanwhile, the stellar flight surgeons put in immense effort to secure all the waivers I needed to resume flying. After an exhaustive series of tests and interviews, I was miraculously granted the necessary waivers. In the interim, I completed my airline transport pilot license. Securing my FAA medical was just as grueling of a process as obtaining the NAMI waivers, but each step brought me closer to my ultimate goal: returning to flight.

At the Strike Fighter Wing Atlantic, I began participating in command PT. My strength was returning, my life was regaining shape, and I was excelling in physical training to the point where I was outpacing most of the command, even with residual nerve damage and four limb-salvaged extremities. My unexpected performance caught the commodore's attention, who commended me on my progress.

*　　　*　　　*

One day at work, the deputy commodore dropped a bombshell: I was to start F/A-18 training at VFA-106. Anticipating a few weeks of preparation, I inquired about the commencement date. His enthusiastic response took me by surprise: "Right now!"

VFA-106, fortunately, shared the same time-worn, leaky hangar as the wing. His news stoked a mix of exhilaration and trepidation in me. It had been a full two years since my ejection, and since waking from my coma, every step had led to this moment. The anticipation was palpable. My only lingering doubt: Could my dormant skills rise to the occasion?

The curriculum of my retraining was akin to the initial ground school, emergency procedure simulators, and flight sessions I had undertaken during my first stint at VFA-106. The instructors, largely supportive of my comeback, included a few familiar faces. Some of my former flight schoolmates had completed their sea tours and returned as instructors themselves.

I noticed an uplifting change in the training environment and morale compared to my previous experience at VFA-106. While the rigorous standards remained the same, the ambience was more conducive to learning. The instructors were far more approachable, and it became easier to ask questions without fear of unwarranted ridicule or chastisement.

The old "Join up and shut up" mentality had transitioned into a new era in the face of ever-evolving tactics and increasingly complex mission capabilities. FNGs were now expected to land at their squadrons, ready to make critical decisions. To do so required instructor mentorship, not just evaluation and harassment.

My retraining journey witnessed steady progress. Despite lingering physical deficits, I was performing exceedingly well. I had managed to adapt to using my nerve-damaged hand for HOTAS controls. There were instances of me limping up the stairwell when nerve pain struck, but I persisted, armed with a smile and unfiltered twisted humor. I wasn't just getting by; I was crushing it, leading to a reserved return of my confidence.

Near the completion of my retraining, a concerning episode unfolded. During a simulated night carrier landing session, I had a mental lapse. My first pass was the best I'd ever flown in

LT Kegan "Smurf" Gill USN (Ret.)

the sim, hitting the target wire precisely, leading to some exceptionally rare praise from the experienced landing signal officer (LSO). But on my second approach, I lost focus and overlooked my radar altimeter setting, a potentially dangerous rookie mistake. The instructor and I were concerned about this isolated, inexplicable event but pressed on, assuming it was an anomaly.

CHAPTER 27

Home on leave in the crisp Michigan winter, fate brought me face-to-face with Cara, a stunning blonde with a smile that could light up even the darkest room. As we stood among mutual friends during the holidays, I felt an instant recognition, realizing that we had crossed paths years before during our college days. Thanks to our friend Pauly, we reconnected, but this time, life aligned our paths in a way that made the connection feel inevitable.

While I was serving in the military, Cara had embarked on a vastly different adventure—one that, in many ways, might have been even more perilous. After working tirelessly as a nurse, she saved up enough to chase the dream of a lifetime, putting her career on hold to travel through Mexico and Central America in a worn-out camper van. Against all advice, even the pleas of border patrol agents who warned her about cartel-controlled areas, Cara ventured forward, undeterred by the dangers. Her journey was marked by countless brushes with danger: corrupt local police, encounters with thieves, crumbling roads, mechanical failures, and the looming shadow of violence. Yet amid the chaos, she encountered vibrant local markets bursting with fresh food, endless kindness of strangers, and lush jungles thriving with life. By the time she returned to the United States, Cara carried with her a deep appreciation for the safety and comfort we often take for granted.

Cara was everything the military had conditioned me to suppress. As a capable nurse, she was grounded in wisdom, but her free-spirited, adventurous soul spoke to a part of me that had long been buried beneath the uniform and rules. Her hippy-pirate outlook on life was exhilarating—a stark contrast to the rigid structure I had grown accustomed to. She wasn't just living life; she was experiencing it in all its raw, unfiltered beauty. Her disdain for the artificial constructs of society and her ability to exist beyond its constraints were a breath of fresh air, and I felt drawn to her authenticity.

One night, under the clear winter starlight of Northern Michigan, as the world around us slowed, I found myself staring into her deep, ocean-blue eyes. We shared our first kiss, and in that moment, something within me awakened that had been dormant for years. It felt as if the warmth of that kiss was melting away layers of rigidity, revealing a part of me I had almost forgotten existed.

As we spent more time together, our connection deepened. Soon, Cara invited me on an adventure that would forever bind us—a two-week sailing trip aboard her parents' refurbished sailboat, *Tiger Sea*, in the Exumas, Bahamas. This was no luxury escape; it was an exploration into the raw beauty of nature, where the tides and winds dictated our days and small mistakes could turn into life-threatening challenges. In this domain of consequences, where I felt the most alive, we truly got to know each other.

Cara and her warm parents guided me as I literally started to learn the ropes. We hunted underwater with spears, where I discovered the tactics and techniques required to hunt with a Hawaiian sling properly. The first time I surfaced with a grouper in hand, her eyes lit up with surprise and admiration. We cooked our fresh catches together, savoring the flavors of the ocean, and spent our nights playing euchre and laughing over sunset margaritas. The gentle lull of the ocean waves rocked us to sleep beneath a blanket of stars, and each night, I felt myself falling deeper for her.

On a tiny, isolated island, with nothing but a single palm tree, the warm waters washing over our feet, and the powdered sugar sand beneath us, we discovered something we hadn't expected—a genuine connection that transcended the chaos of our pasts. Cara's initial hesitations about dating someone in the military melted away as we realized how beautifully our worlds intertwined. Together, we had found a love that was as adventurous, unpredictable and free-spirited as the journey that brought us there.

*   *   *

As I completed my retraining at VFA-106, Cara relocated to join me in Virginia Beach and started working as a trauma nurse in Virginia Beach General's frequently chaotic emergency department. Her days were filled with gunshot wounds, endless vehicle traumas, overdoses, and transient psychotic mental health patients. Although incredibly stressful, Cara thrived and quickly became a valued, talented department member.

Cara and I along with a handful of our fun-loving Oceanfront surf crew catching some Outer Banks swell circa 2016.

She integrated seamlessly into our vibrant, spontaneous, huck 'n' buck, surf-loving Oceanfront crew. During our free time, we would grab our boards and ride our beach cruisers down to the ocean. Cara, our enchanting mermaid, seemed to have a special connection with the sea creatures, as we often surfed among playful dolphins whenever she paddled out with us.

As the year passed, it was evident that she was the woman I wanted to spend the rest of my life with. In the spirit of light-hearted chivalry, I proposed to her with a Ring Pop. She accepted, and we began planning a simple but heartfelt backyard wedding in Michigan.

Our informal ceremony took place against the stunning backdrop of Northern Michigan's lush, glacier-carved hills, attended by a small gathering of our nearest and dearest. Our adventurous friend Pauly, responsible for our reacquaintance, presided over the proceedings as an ordained Dudeist priest after completing an intense, fifteen-minute online course. Under the soothing warmth of the September sun, White Russian in hand, he joined us in matrimony. The celebration of our union kicked off with an abundance of home-cooked gumbo and an open bar, setting the tone for joyful festivities.

*   *   *

Defying all odds and my injuries, I graduated at the top of my class, earning the Top Stick Award. I was also bestowed with the River Rat Award, acknowledging who brought the most fun outside the cockpit.

VFA-136 Knighthawks in Lemoore, California, circa 2017.

At the patching ceremony, our fleet squadrons were revealed. While we had hoped to remain in Virginia Beach, where Cara and I had become part of a tight-knit crew, the navy had other plans. I was assigned to the VFA-136 Knighthawks at NAS Lemoore in California. While this move posed a challenge for our new marriage, I was accustomed to the navy's requirements and was grateful to return to a fleet squadron after everything I had been through. Cara was no stranger to travel, so we packed up and headed west. The challenges our marriage would face were just beginning.

CHAPTER 28

NAS Lemoore is nestled in the heart of California's Central Valley. The locals were friendly, but the environment was less so. The air and water were heavily polluted. If you've seen the film *Erin Brockovich*, starring Julia Roberts, you have an idea of the water issues in the region. A behemoth corporation neglected to install appropriate liners in their waste discharge ponds, resulting in toxic chemicals leaking into the groundwater. The resultant pollution causes serious health complications if consumed or bathed over an extended period.

We devised a macabre game as we drove through the haze that enveloped the decaying farmland: "Guess that smell." The persistent mix of animal waste and the chemical stench was an unfortunate part of our daily lives, with each shift in the wind direction bringing a new, nauseating odor.

From the cockpit of the F-18, I was able to climb above the haze to witness the splendor of Sequoia National Park and Yosemite. Despite the desolation of the Central Valley, these natural wonders were within easy reach. Cara and I would escape on the rare free weekend to explore these parks.

The sensory assault of the Central Valley melted away as we journeyed toward Big Sur. As we descended from the clouds enveloping the mountain, we were met with the stunning vista of the untouched coastline. The dramatic cliffs, the mighty Pacific Ocean, and the refreshing sea breeze were welcome changes from our daily environment. We surfed in some of the most secluded spots in California, sharing the water with the silent silhouettes of the "men in gray suits"—the sharks—who seemed content to keep to themselves.

*   *   *

Continuing my duties in the understaffed VFA-136, an unsettling trend emerged. I found it increasingly difficult to retain new information. Tasks that I once completed with ease turned into daily battles, and recovery from my workouts took much longer than before. Years of pushing my damaged body to its limits had begun to show significant effects. Though I didn't know it at the time, the high-stress environment of the squadron was aggravating my unresolved traumatic brain injury (TBI) from the ejection. I became an intermittent curmudgeon, the opposite of my typical lighthearted demeanor.

To maintain my waning concentration, I constantly refilled my coffee cup. When that no longer did the trick, I turned to tobacco snus pouches to stay alert during study sessions. Sleep began to evade me, and whiskey on the rocks turned from an occasional indulgence to a necessity for a night's rest. The substances I once typically used in celebration became a daily requirement.

An upcoming detachment to Tyndall Air Force Base in Florida for live fire weapons training brought excitement. I looked forward to the opportunity to fire an actual AIM-9M Sidewinder missile at a drone, followed by the chance to join up with an F-22 Raptor from the National Guard's 199th Fighter Squadron for dissimilar air combat training (DACT). This would essentially be a dogfight—navy versus air force. The Raptor pilots, based out of Pearl Harbor, were privileged to fly the world's most formidable fighter jet and spent their weekends surfing on Oahu's pristine North Shore—a dream job. However, my enthusiasm quickly dampened when we almost missed the briefing.

Finding the briefing location was more challenging than anticipated, even with our executive officer, Blue, leading the way. We interrupted after the squared-away Raptor pilots began their briefing, missing some crucial details. The brief highlighted the drastic difference in operational languages between the air force and the navy. Despite the confusion, I was eager to walk to the jet (or "step," as the air force calls it).

Our pre-flight preparation was unusually chaotic due to our late arrival and the need to adjust to the air force's timeline. My squadron mate Quitter and I scrambled to gear up to get our jets up and running on time. As I started my engines, the mission lead initiated the radio check-in. As Murphy's Law would have it, my radios malfunctioned, causing me to miss the check-in while manually entering the required frequencies for the flight. With roughly a dozen jets ready to fly, nobody was going to wait for me. Spotting my flight lead taxiing for takeoff, I quickly rushed through my weapons checks to catch up. My primary mission was to fire the live AIM-9M Sidewinder on my wing. Despite the chaos, I took off on time and completed the day's mission.

The legendary *Star Wars* canyon along the R-2508 Sidewinder low-level route in California. Photographers often perch themselves along the route to capture these incredible shots.

Watching my tapes after the flight, I was troubled by my inability to remember much of the missile shoot. Yet despite the fragmented memories, certain moments remained clear. I still remember the awe I felt watching the Raptor perform its maneuvers up close, its directional thrust defying the standard laws of fighter aerodynamics. I remembered the flight back, the Raptor pilot's words still echoing.

"The Raptor makes even mediocre pilots look good," he'd said, which I had initially taken as a humble remark. That illusion was quickly shattered when he keyed his mic again, confidently stating, "But I don't have that problem."

At precisely 299 knots, I flew on his wing for the slowest overhead break I'd ever flown. The "fun police" over at the air force were even stricter than those at the navy, revoking their privilege to a high-speed break.

The prospect of having such gaping memory blanks after firing a live, heat-seeking missile was disconcerting. Nevertheless, I chalked it up to exhaustion and assumed a decent night's sleep would help. However, rest didn't come easy that night, and the next day brought more challenges. I did my best to suck it up.

As the squadron duty officer (SDO) that day, I was tasked with simple responsibilities like answering phone calls and coordinating the flight schedule. When I returned to my hotel room that evening, I was grappling with a disturbing sensation—I was experiencing vertigo for the first time. The room seemed to pulsate beneath me. Even setting my alarm for the following day proved a struggle as I couldn't perform the simple math required. I tried to open the calculator on my phone to do the no-brainer arithmetic but struggled to operate it. My mind was racing, and relaxing seemed to be an impossible feat.

Multiple type II decompression sickness (DCS) incidents were reported within the Hornet and Super Hornet communities during this period. The pressurization system of these aircraft was causing rapid fluctuations in cabin pressure, a situation akin to scuba divers ascending too quickly from a deep dive. This rapid decompression could lead to the formation of tiny nitrogen bubbles in the bloodstream, similar to how bubbles form in a beer bottle when popped open.

Type I DCS, also known as "the bends," occurs when these nitrogen bubbles form in a joint, leading to painful aches. In contrast, Type II DCS occurs when these bubbles form in the brain. The symptoms can range from cognitive impairments, like memory loss and lack of focus, to more severe symptoms that mimic a stroke or an aneurysm. If left untreated, type II DCS can be fatal, as the bubbles can disrupt circulation to the brain. Recent cases had rendered some aircrew incapacitated, permanently trapped in a vegetative state following such malfunctions. The need to fix the pressurization system was a community-wide priority, but the time it took to implement a solution led to further injuries among the aircrew.

The uncertainty and anxiety of knowing something was wrong but being unable to identify it was torturous. I reached out to the squadron safety officer, Squeezer. He was the same pilot who instructed my first flight in the Super Hornet years ago, now helping me after what might have been my last. He drove me to the nearby Mayport dive base, which housed a hyperbaric chamber for treating DCS.

The navy dive center physician wasn't entirely sure what was wrong, but we agreed to proceed with the hyperbaric chamber treatment. Given my foggy cognitive function, I felt I had no option but to take a chance at a potential solution.

As I lay inside the hyperbaric chamber, a dive corpsman accompanying me started to share tales of their missions. He spoke of grueling weeks spent working hundreds of feet below the sea, their only respite being a cramped capsule where they ate and slept between dives. It was a world far removed from my experience in the air, yet the parallels were clear: Both professions required us to push beyond our physical limitations, endure harsh conditions, and grapple with the dangerous unpredictability of our environments.

One particular gruesome story he shared caught my attention. He spoke of instances where the hyperbaric chamber had malfunctioned, rapidly decompressing and causing a violent expansion of every air molecule inside its occupants. The vivid description of those unfortunate service members turned into a "dripping pink goo" was disturbing. Such tales were not exactly comforting at the moment but still captivating.

Despite the unsettling stories, the hyperbaric chamber treatment provided some relief. After about three and a half hours, I noticed my mind was clearing up slightly. The physician decided he would need to see me again the next day. My concerned commanding officer, Whep, drove me back to the hotel, where I hoped to find sleep, but my mind and heart continued to race. The uncertainty was troubling, and I couldn't shake the feeling that something was wrong.

The next day, I returned to the physician at Mayport dive base and explained that while the hyperbaric treatment had brought some relief, it was far from a miracle cure. I still wasn't back to normal. He suggested I consult the flight surgeon once I return to NAS Lemoore.

During the trip home, I started experiencing bouts of paranoia. I was convinced that someone had planted classified materials in my carry-on, attempting to set me up. The unsettling thoughts were difficult to control, but I managed to keep them at bay, aware at some level that they were irrational.

The trip back also involved a surprisingly challenging game of Words with Friends with my squadron mate, call sign Choda Boy, named after a movie character with a floppy dildo stuck to his forehead. Simple three-letter words were perplexing to me as if they were complex puzzles. The extent of my cognitive impairment wasn't entirely clear at the time; I was too confused to appreciate the gravity of my condition thoroughly.

Back in California, sleep remained a stubborn adversary. I found myself reluctantly leaning on the support of a compassionate flight surgeon at the base. My reluctance stemmed from the fear that another medical involvement might jeopardize my flying career. Yet I understood that if I didn't seek help, my compromised mental state could endanger my life and others. I didn't want to become a liability. With a heavy heart, I proceeded to come clean about my struggles.

Soon, the flight surgeon recommended that I consult with the psychology department. The focus of our conversations quickly shifted to my emotional inconsistencies, and I found myself in long, awkward discussions about my feelings.

Eventually, they diagnosed me with delayed onset post-traumatic stress disorder (PTSD). Their proposed initial treatment? A variety of therapeutic apps on my phone. I found it almost laughable that their first "serious" suggestion to treat my complex condition was some apps. These included a cognitive processing therapy app (CPT) and a cognitive behavioral therapy app (CBT). The weekly meetings with the psychologist to discuss these apps only increased my frustration.

In retrospect, my symptoms distinctly pointed toward traumatic brain injury (TBI). However, considering my complex medical history and the limited resources available in Lemoore, my treatment pathway was filled with more prescription drugs. Despite my reluctance to start another medication regimen, given my previous bouts with withdrawal symptoms, the doctors gave no other viable options.

I finally mustered up the courage to confidentially discuss my future as a pilot with my command. My executive officer, Blue, expressed concern about the psychology department having "sunk their talons into me." At that time, I didn't fully understand his concern, but it became painfully clear in hindsight. Seeking mental health assistance doomed my flying career, and the psychotropic drugs were the talons that would carry me to my demise.

For several months, I voluntarily managed responsibilities as a squadron duty officer and wrote the flight schedule while grappling with additional assessments and treatments from the psychology department. I was grounded, and the sensation of letting down my already understaffed squadron ate at me relentlessly. I took on various ground jobs, attempting to alleviate some of the burdens from my squadron mates, but the persistent guilt of feeling like I was letting my brothers down was a constant irritant.

Cloaked in my freshly cut hair, clean flight suit, and polished brown Redwing boots, I hoped that my external appearance could sufficiently conceal the depth of my struggle beneath the surface. My uniform was my armor, shielding the world from the raw turmoil I was experiencing internally. This period was one of the toughest in my life, navigating a labyrinth of mental health assessments and trying to uphold my responsibilities while wrestling with the guilt of feeling like I was not contributing enough to my squadron. Amid the uncertainty, Cara and I had a baby on the way. My struggles starkly contrasted with the confident and put-together image I hoped my uniform projected. I was desperate to hide my pain, hoping no one could see the severe difficulties I was dealing with beneath the surface. I began receding from my squadron mates, ashamed of myself.

I was becoming a serious burden on Cara as she worked tirelessly to coordinate with the psychology department to keep me from being hospitalized. As my mental state deteriorated, I could no longer safely operate a motor vehicle—another weight on Cara's back.

Sleep was becoming my worst enemy. The worsening insomnia was driving me towards heightened paranoia and hypervigilance. I recall experiencing a strange sense of being in *The Truman Show*. Ordinary people seemed like hired actors. I started reading messages in the songs on the radio, feeling like they were trying to manipulate my emotions. Such symptoms are not uncommon for people dealing with brain injuries and sleep deprivation. While I could initially shake it off and realign with reality, the psychiatrist introduced a potent psychotropic drug called quetiapine into my regimen.

Originally conceived as an antipsychotic, quetiapine, or Seroquel as it is commonly known, was initially prescribed in low doses to tackle my persistent insomnia. Many of these symptoms would fade if I could get a good night's sleep.

Even at the low starting dosage, quetiapine floored me. I spent the days trapped in a vortex of fatigue, devoid of desire to do anything. But it did provide the relief of unconsciousness at night. However, a critical difference exists between drug-induced blackout and rejuvenating restful sleep. It masked my symptoms effectively enough for a short while to make me believe it was working, seemingly validating the psychiatrist's years of education. However, as with all pharmaceuticals, my body developed a tolerance, necessitating an increase in dosage. As the dosage climbed, the side effects followed suit.

Meanwhile, the damage to my brain's physiology caused by the underlying unresolved TBI was only aggravated. The quetiapine merely offered a temporary veil over the real issue. The psychiatrist continued to be stumped, prescribing more drugs and suggesting fanciful visualizations of flowers or waterfalls to make my problems vanish. No surprise, this was less than helpful.

Despite several more months of therapy and medication, my mental faculties deteriorated. I was transferred from the Knighthawks to the West Coast version of the Land of Misfit Toys at Strike Fighter Wing Pacific—a clear indication that my flying career was reaching its twilight. My condition made reporting to work an arduous task. Even a simple desk job with minimal responsibilities triggered panic attacks. Part of me was mortified at the thought of being confined to the drab office, making copies and brewing coffee for the remainder of my service. My day-to-day life turned into a nightmare, with symptoms of psychosis on the rise.

CHAPTER 29

My friend Leo, a special amphibious reconnaissance corps-man (SARC) out of Naval Station Dam Neck, gifted me a block of East Indian rosewood he'd "acquired" during a deployment right before I moved away from Virginia Beach. The wood was incredibly hard, just like the environment it came from. Leo's gift ignited my therapeutic hobby of woodworking. I started turning smoking pipes on a small lathe, creating gifts for my squadron mates while wrestling with my internal struggles.

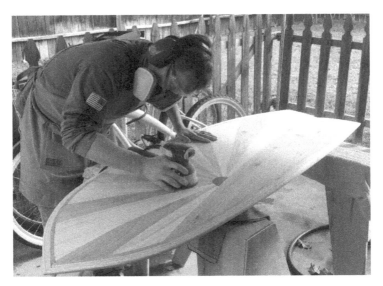

Building a hollow wooden surfboard for my good friend Vinny.

Eventually, my skills evolved, and I began carving fully functional hollow wooden surfboards. The process required intense focus and hands-on work, effectively distracting me from my unraveling life. Crafting something tangible and complex helped me maintain a semblance of control during immense uncertainty.

Catching some swell at Morro Bay, California, with Operation Surf.

During these testing times, I stumbled upon the documentary *Resurface*. The film follows the journey of a US Marine named Bobby, who, while grappling with PTSD/TBI, discovers healing and tranquility through surfing alongside big wave surfing legend Laird Hamilton, an initiative supported by Operation Surf. The organization, established by another big wave surfing legend, Van Curaza, aspires to expose veterans to the ocean's therapeutic prowess.

Motivated by this revelation, I connected with Operation Surf in Santa Cruz. They embraced me warmly, making me feel like a valuable part of their community. Like military personnel, the courageous spirits of professional surfers are drawn to a life that teeters on the edge. The inherent risks often result in injuries akin to those service members suffer. The healing I found in the ocean, amplified by the Operation Surf crew's buoyant spirits, briefly lifted my mental and physical wellness. This was markedly more effective than any clinical therapy I had undergone in Lemoore. Immersing in the ocean, surfing the waves, and being part of a supportive community gave me peace and resilience amid the chaos. Nature, indeed, is a healer.

Surfing and woodworking were at least a sip of fresh air before my worsening mental health struggles crushed me deeper beneath the surface than I had ever experienced, into the depths where light no longer penetrates.

CHAPTER 30

The psychology department began the proceedings to medically discharge me from military service. By this point, I was so worn out and exasperated by my deteriorating condition that I wanted to be alone. I had fought tooth and nail to reclaim my place in the cockpit, supported every step of the way by the strike fighter community. Numerous physicians had advocated for me, ensuring my waivers were approved. Countless dollars had been poured into my training. The weight of disappointing everyone who had put their faith in me was crushing.

I began the medical board process by connecting with my physical evaluation board liaison officer, or PEBLO. She had recently stepped into the position, which had been vacant for more than half a year. The first time we met, I found her office inundated with disorganized stacks of paperwork covering every surface. As I stood in her office, she spent most of our designated meeting time on the phone with her daughter, casually discussing college roommate antics. My frustration bubbled beneath the surface. It was evident that Cara and I would have to navigate this burdensome process independently. The PEBLO proved less than helpful, a constant source of frustration as my case slowly advanced.

My paranoia escalated to an unbearable degree. I started believing government assassins were pursuing me. A casual stroll to the tranquil park a few blocks from our house became an ordeal as I became convinced that strangers were undercover agents observing me and biding their time. Even though these thoughts were irrational, they became my reality. Fear gripped me at seeing windows in our house, believing a sniper might be lying in wait. I suspected our food and water were poisoned and, consequently, stopped eating and drinking. The government *was* poisoning me, but it was in the form of FDA-approved psychotropic medication prescribed to me by the indoctrinated lab coats.

My demeanor and physical appearance changed drastically. Once vibrant, my eyes looked hollow and recessed into my face. My skin appeared pale and lifeless as my muscles started to atrophy. The man in the mirror seemed like a stranger. Yet my wife somehow found the strength to manage me as I disintegrated, considering our newborn son's needs a more straightforward task.

Late one dreary night, in the grip of a suffocating depression, I reached for the end table next to my bed, where I stored my handgun. My broken mind began painting a grim picture—imagining the cold touch of the barrel against my teeth, the taste of gun oil on my tongue. I felt I had let down everyone who believed in me. Now I was just a washed-up failure. All I wanted was to escape from the relentless physical and emotional agony. I was mere moments away from inserting the barrel into my mouth when I glanced at my wife, peacefully sleeping beside our newborn son. The sight of them stirred something within me, a flicker of light in the oppressive darkness. I pictured the horrific scene they'd wake up to, the remnants of my life violently splattered on the adjacent wall. I quietly closed the drawer and laid down next to them, silent tears streaming down my face. Their presence in that critical moment saved me from the irreversible decision countless other veterans succumb to when left hopelessly broken. Had I been alone, I would have joined the over forty-four veterans killing themselves by suicide or overdose each day.

The psychology team at the base recognized the severity of my condition and began discussing potential options for inpatient treatment with Cara. Despite the clear need for additional assistance, she went to great lengths to avoid my admission into a mental institution. Cara knew from her previous experience dealing with mental health patients in the emergency department how mismanaged inpatient psych facilities were.

The usually simple task of grocery shopping became a burdensome half-day affair as I was constantly convinced each stranger who passed through the aisles was trying to assassinate me. She wanted better for me but was already busy with our newborn son, so she recruited my parents to fly out and help.

There were moments when my imagination took such a stronghold that reality became blurred. I could not distinguish between what was real and merely a fabrication of my mind. My life had become a perpetual nightmare, a harrowing blend of wakefulness and illusion. Looking back, I can differentiate between reality and the surreal dreamscape I was trapped in, but back then, my waking life was overpowered by an ever-encroaching waking nightmare.

Some of my hallucinations, however, were exhilarating. I started imagining that my wife was the real-life Carrie Mathison, the character from the series *Homeland*. Given Cara's resemblance to the blonde fictional CIA agent featured in the show, my mind began weaving a story where she was on a mission to rescue me from sinister government agents hellbent on my execution. I believed the entire show was based on my wife's actual life and built a narrative reinforcing my delusions.

As Cara drove me to an appointment at the Fresno Veterans Affairs hospital, where they were to assess my conditions for a VA disability rating, my delusions took over. As I gazed out the window, road signs appeared to transform into secret messages explicitly meant for me. I was convinced I was developing superhuman powers and being drafted to become a covert operative. My wife, supposedly working for the CIA, had vouched for me, and my current struggles were part of the trials I had to overcome to discover my newfound abilities. My mind concocted a story surrounding my ejection to substantiate my secret agent fantasy. I believed that my ejection was part of a convoluted test to evaluate my fitness for this elite group of white-hat government operatives.

At the VA hospital, I was evaluated for a multitude of injuries. Despite having a disc containing all my medical records that clearly suggested a case for medical retirement, my assessment was brief and dismissive. The cantankerous VA neurologist refused to let my wife into the room while he conducted his facade of an evaluation. Once we were alone, he took out a small tool resembling a prickly pizza cutter and rapidly rolled it along my exposed arms. He curtly stated that I had no significant damage and dismissed me in just a few minutes. No assessment was performed for TBI. As I exited the room, surprised by the absurdly short review, Cara exclaimed, "That's it?" As much as I wished this was a figment of my imagination, Cara confirmed it was the genuine treatment I received at the VA.

Even with the extensive documentation of injuries undoubtedly sustained during my service and the support of my command and the medical staff on base, the medical board process was a clusterfuck I wouldn't wish upon anyone except the bumbling bureaucrats that designed it. I couldn't fathom going through this process as a junior enlisted service member.

The cumbersome procedure needed to complete a medical board can be likened to the bureaucratic version of the Temple of Doom. Each step of the process is fraught with pitfalls and complications. My incompetent PEBLO ceased returning our calls, and I was often treated as though my afflictions were feigned. Most of the VA doctors did not take the time to review my medical records or conduct comprehensive assessments thoroughly. Thankfully, one VA doctor went above and beyond to ensure that most of my muscular injuries were evaluated correctly. My situation could have been considerably worse had it not been for him.

At the start of the process, the remote legal representative assigned to me regarded my case as a "red cow," an undeniable instance warranting medical retirement. He assured me that, given the clear evidence in my case, the process should be uncomplicated and straightforward. However, burdened with over three thousand cases a year, our interactions were limited to brief phone calls, with no in-person meetings. Despite his review of every document before submission, errors occurred that necessitated an appeal on my part. The arduous process seemed intentionally designed to undermine the disabled service member.

With the PEBLO continually misplacing my paperwork, my frustrations steadily mounted. What was meant to take a maximum of six months dragged on for a year and a half. This entire period was an ordeal for Cara, who found herself raising our newborn single-handedly, looking after me in my dysfunctional state, and navigating the nightmare of the medical board process. Her sweet demeanor and glowing optimism managed to persevere. I don't know how she did it.

A single form completed at the outset of the medical board process failed to encompass all my injuries, leading to only one ailment, PTSD, being considered when determining my final disability rating. Despite piles of medical records and various documents making a clear, concise case for medical retirement, the only document considered by the jaded board members was one line on that single piece of paper. Even though my severe symptoms, including psychosis, were documented, I was rated as if my PTSD was only mild to moderate. To rectify these glaring errors, I had to appeal the rating decision, which involved traveling across the country to meet the medical board in person.

Proud father to my newborn son. My flight suit and clean appearance masked the internal struggles raging beneath the surface.

Cara, our baby boy, and I traveled to Washington, DC, to discover our family's future. Having just undergone another surgery at Stanford, I relied on my old wooden cane to navigate without tripping over my salvaged legs. I could hear Aunt Smuggs's comically chiding voice in my head, giving me hell about that cane. My summer white uniform, adorned with this cane and the long red scars visible on my bare forearms, held more significance than any of the ribbons on my chest.

Holding my head high, I faced the three high-ranking military members tasked with deciding my family's fate. The room had a formal, almost punitive, setup. As I stood at attention before the trio, it felt like a disciplinary hearing. The board members briefly questioned me from their elevated platform, eyes drilling into me. The room was thick with tension.

One of the board members, a hefty E-9 pilot, seemed convinced I was crafting a grand scheme to exit the military and secure a job with a commercial airline. Had he even glanced at my medical records, it would have been evident that securing the FAA first-class medical certification required to be an airline transport pilot was far from feasible. Moreover, I had no interest in flying on autopilot with a bus full of disgruntled, sardined passengers and overbearing flight attendants instead of blasting through the sky in nimble fighter jets.

The stern medical officer on the board intermittently perused my file silently, shooting me judgmental glances over his thick glasses like I had concocted the records in front of him. The room felt void of air. A tangible silence fell over the board members as they deliberated. It felt like time had come to a standstill, much like the moment just before I pulled the ejection handle.

Finally, the steely-eyed marine lieutenant colonel on the panel broke the silence. "You served your country honorably and were injured in the line of duty. Please enjoy your military retirement with your beautiful family. Thank you for your service."

The decision could have easily swayed the other way with a slightly different panel. I could have ended up homeless in the DC area, living under an overpass, like many forgotten veterans whose board reviews didn't favor them. Countless veterans who have done far more in their service than I ever did, suffering from worse injuries, struggling to survive and frequently perishing on the streets of the most wealthy nation on earth.

*　　*　　*

We found ourselves back in Lemoore, awaiting my final orders, anticipating the move to Michigan, where we could lean on the much-needed support of our families. My unpredictably erratic behavior required constant supervision, so Cara took me for a grocery run at the base commissary. The moment we stepped inside, it felt as though every stranger's gaze was fixed on me, their eyes appearing large, menacingly black, their teeth protruding grotesquely. They resembled sinister creatures from a nightmare, their gaze relentlessly tracking my every move within the commissary. Fighting to keep my composure, my heart hammered away in my chest as I strived to ignore the terrifying faces that seemed to shadow me persistently.

As we moved to checkout, the woman bagging our groceries extended her hand, presumably for a tip. Through my distorted perspective, she appeared like a shackled being reaching out to drain my soul, using it as a lifeline for her deliverance. I could feel my vitality draining as I imagined my soul, visualized as a wispy plume of fog, being extracted to nourish this bound demon charged with bagging our provisions. Overwhelmed with fear, I remained frozen as my wife gently led me away. She managed to usher me and our son into the car, and we left the base.

Glancing into the rearview mirror, I watched as the entire naval base seemed to rip away from the ground behind us. It rose slowly into the air, chunks of concrete, dirt, and rebar crumbling away from beneath. A gaping black chasm had opened underneath the levitating base, a horrifying abyss leading straight to hell.

CHAPTER 31

For countless grueling months, the relentless ticking of the clock served as a grim reminder of my impending medical retirement. After an arduous eighteen-month journey through medical board evaluations, paperwork drills, and countless complications, my military service tenure ended. Faced with looming uncertainty and a deep-seated longing for the familiar, my wife and I decided to relocate to Northern Michigan, where our families resided. Our lives teetered on the edge of instability. My wife relentlessly found herself burdened with the role of being my primary caregiver, while I felt increasingly lost in a sea of rage, frustration, and worsening depression.

Despite our earnest efforts to seek aid from the VA caregiver program, our appeals were repeatedly dismissed. This program was designed to provide financial support to a spouse forced to give up their livelihood to cater to the demanding needs of a debilitated service member. Given our circumstances, we thought we would certainly qualify, yet, like so many others in search of assistance from the VA, we were consistently turned away.

In my pursuit of recovery, I found myself under the watchful eyes of a psychologist and a psychiatrist from the VA. Their solution to my tumultuous internal chaos was a lifelong prescription of quetiapine, posing as a psychological panacea. Caught in a perpetual imbalance, I was either a hollow shell or on the precipice of psychosis. The vibrant hues of my personality and humor had been dulled, replaced by a constant irritation that snapped at the slightest triggers. As my body adapted to the medication, my dependence grew stronger, increasing the dosage to induce poor-quality sleep.

An audacious leap in my prescribed dosage of quetiapine—from 300 to 450 milligrams per night—plunged me into the deepest recesses of psychosis yet. My faculties abandoned me at home. My mother was playing guardian to my son as Cara attended a job interview. When Cara returned, she found me having hacked off large chunks of my hair, shorn off my eyebrows, and face bare. Draped in nothing but a black plastic garbage bag fashioned like a cape, resembling a disheveled Bruce Wayne after a rough night out in Gotham, I was ready to battle invisible villains.

A desperate call to the VA resulted in the grim announcement of an impending police visit. A patrol car rolled into our driveway, and a baffled patrolman approached. Cara interjected, unwilling to subject me to being cuffed in my vulnerable state. Drawing from her experiences with psych patients during her ER nurse tenure, she took charge. She ordered me into comfortable clothes and cautioned me to ditch the shoelaces from my shoes, preparing for the inevitable confinement at the hospital.

As Cara and my mom busied themselves preparing for the impending hospital visit, I was lost in my own world, crafting what I thought was a lasso out of discarded shoelaces. I was caught in a delusional cowboy fantasy. My son, fastened in his infant car seat, ready for our hour-long trip to the ER, sat with a noose of shoelace looped loosely around his neck. To me, it was harmless, a game where I was the hero. But when Cara returned, she was met with a scene far more sinister—a potentially dangerous trap created by a man she no longer recognized.

The sight of her son, entangled in a makeshift noose, with me standing there gripping the other end like a madman, was a blow to her heart—a scalpel slicing through what was left of the trust we once built. I wasn't the capable man she once knew. In that moment, I had become something darker, a threat to the very child I loved most. Her shock turned quickly to action. In a heartbeat, she pulled me away from the fantasy world I had sunk into, sweeping me toward the car and loading our son into the back seat. Both Cara and my mom were shaken by what could have been.

Even in the depths of psychosis, where reality blurred and madness reigned, I still recognized Cara's voice. Her directives were clear and firm yet laced with a gentleness that cut through the fog clouding my mind. At that moment, she wasn't just my partner—she was my anchor, her presence glowing with a calm that belied the terror of the situation. To me, she appeared angelic, radiating a light that I could follow out of the chaos I had created.

Without resistance, I followed her lead, getting into the car as if nothing had happened, as if the madness was just another fleeting moment in a sea of confusion. But for Cara, the weight of what had just transpired lingered heavily. She had seen the man she loved, the father of her child, teeter on the brink of becoming something dangerous. The pain in her heart was palpable, yet she steered the car with the steady resolve of someone who knew that the man she loved was still somewhere within me, waiting to be saved.

Our journey to the hospital had me under the illusory grip of a nuclear catastrophe, the mirror reflecting an apocalyptic mushroom cloud sprouting in the distance behind us. Nature's fury enveloped us as skies darkened ominously and violent lightning cracked around us. Boats, trees, defenseless wildlife, and debris swirled in the tempestuous air created by my out-of-control imagination. The winding roads echoed our desperate flight from the phantom shockwave, excitement and terror boiling within me. An hour later, we halted in front of the emergency room.

As I stepped out of the car, the storm faded. Brazenly, I relieved myself in a nearby potted plant, oblivious to onlookers. An incredulous security guard approached hastily, only to be intercepted by my mother. As Cara tended to our son, my mom, the negotiator, explained my hallucinatory state. His pompous retort about witnessing worse did nothing but incense her. She demanded medical assistance, not incarceration, and ultimately, he relented, allowing me passage into the ER. My mother's scrappiness saved the day.

Guided by my mom, I checked in and was soon taken in by the staff. Bathroom permission was granted but with the caveat of an unlocked door. My disappearance into the restroom extended beyond the necessary, and the subsequent investigation found me stark naked in a trash can. With my mother's aid, the staff relocated me to a room.

Reality slipped through my fingers as an ethereal journey yanked me out of my body. I embodied the first atom, time-traveling from the dawn of existence to the distant future. A cosmic slideshow unraveled, depicting the chronicles of the universe. An imagined rendezvous with my father, a fellow time traveler in prehistoric times, left me with a fleeting smile before he evaporated into his journey. His departure plunged me into an unsettling solitude reminiscent of a spaceman spinning out of control in a capsule lost in the cosmos.

Gradually, I phased back into my physical existence, yet my mind remained in disarray. When my mom visited, she found me entranced by the TV; my gaze was fixated on its relentless sputter of monochrome static. With a twisted grin and an uncanny cadence in my voice, I kept gesturing toward the screen, rapidly alternating my gaze between her and the TV, exclaiming in ominous, staccato repetition, "Do you see that? Do you see that? DO YOU SEE THAT!" In the labyrinth of my psychosis, I believed I was wielding the remote to flip through the epochs of the past and the impending future. Each click whisked me from medieval knights to Neanderthals, dinosaurs, and more. Clicking upward from the present, I visualized a dystopian future dominated by multinational corporations. I saw humanity manipulated into manic consumerism, drowning in piles of garbage and toxic air, inciting universal insanity. My hallucinations presented me with a news anchor, their plastered grin eerily incongruent with the disturbing report, mirroring the calm amidst the chaos. As I continued to flip through this dystopian future, I witnessed the downfall of civilization into a nuclear war. The sight of her son, once full of life, now trapped in the relentless grip of madness, was a heartbreaking spectacle for my mother.

The emergency department, ill-equipped to handle prolonged psych patient care, started exploring alternative accommodations. The surrounding inpatient psych facilities were overwhelmed. Upon discovering my veteran status, the choice veered towards a VA inpatient psych facility in Battle Creek, Michigan. Sedated and confused, I was strapped into an ambulance for the four-hour drive south. My delirious imagination had me thinking I popped the cap on the green oxygen canister strapped to my gurney, triggering a blast and liberating me into highway traffic on my rocket-powered backboard. However, reality saw me drooling and staring vacantly at the ceiling of the moving vehicle.

CHAPTER 32

My earliest recollection of the Battle Creek facility was of awakening on the chilly, hard floor, clad in what seemed like a blood-soaked diaper. I had the horrific impression of being in a dark prison cell with my testicles gruesomely removed. Probing my diaper, I felt greasy, warm blood and what I believed to be remnants of mutilated flesh. A pair of eyes peeked through the small door window before it snapped shut abruptly, and I faded back into unconsciousness.

Subsequently, a figure in a white lab coat materialized in my room. He bore an uncanny resemblance to my college roommate's father, Tom. In my delirium, I surmised that Tom had infiltrated this place as an undercover psychiatrist with a mission to liberate me from my predicament. As the fog of psychosis ebbed and flowed, periods of clarity began to penetrate my delusions. Time became an elusive concept as I languished in that room. Gradually regaining strength, I hoisted myself to my feet and was relieved to find my testicles intact. The door, surprisingly unlocked, beckoned me to venture out and explore the facility.

Emerging from the dim room, the bright, stark-white hallway greeted me, lending me an illusory height of ten feet. Each footstep thundered, echoing off the sterile tiles, and I felt like a towering giant lumbering into the common area, the vibrations reverberating through the building. Furnished with a large flat-screen TV, rows of cushioned seats, and multiple round dining tables, the common area was populated by a motley crew of veterans. I had shrunk back to my usual size by the time I entered.

The spectrum of the facility's inhabitants ranged from seemingly regular vets playing cards to an older, scraggly man pacing the halls, mumbling and shouting in nervous agitation. A lively character, reminiscent of Doc from *Back to the Future*, cracked jokes and taught me a peculiar trick of teeth whitening using Styrofoam. A portly man with an insatiable appetite tore into his snacks like Cookie Monster before stomping away, grumbling under his breath. A gentle, elderly man proposed an unconventional method of snack consumption—upside down, which he earnestly recommended I try.

A supervised, compact room offered basic amenities: a sink, a refrigerator, a drip coffee machine, and two towering cylinders dispensing artificially sweetened beverages. The veterans could satiate their thirst with either red or yellow concoctions. The tap water was reminiscent of an abandoned hot tub, an overpowering blend of chlorine and minerals that made even the artificial raspberry lemonade unpalatable. A solitary computer, nestled within a plexiglass enclosure, provided limited internet access for shared patient use. However, it was often monopolized by a vacant-eyed veteran, who found solace in endlessly spinning the reels on a free slot machine game.

Sleep within the facility was a scarce commodity despite the arsenal of sedatives at our disposal. The tortured cries and incoherent murmurs of other distressed veterans punctuated the night, reverberating ominously through the silent corridors. The rhythmical clatter of patrol staff and the jingle of their keys frequently roused me from my fleeting bouts of slumber. Their flashlights routinely pierced the darkness of my room as they peered through the small window in my door. While most of the understaffed personnel were kindhearted, a few seemed to disregard the fundamental human dignity of their patients. A particular staff member seemed to fancy herself a stern authoritarian rather than a caregiver.

In her sixties, with impeccably maintained white-blonde hair, she exhibited an extravagant necklace featuring a cluster of gold the size of a walnut. The dynamics of our relationship eerily mirrored those in the Stanford prison experiment. She donned the white lab coat, while I was outfitted in baggy prison scrubs and flip-flops. To her, we veterans appeared to be mere troublemakers, and she seemed to relish asserting her control over us through subtle cruelties.

Whenever other staff members were around, the draconian matron I nicknamed "Goldy" would put on a facade of benevolence, creating an illusion of her being a compassionate and caring individual. But as soon as she knew she was out of their sight, dealing with patients suffering from different levels of psychosis, her true colors would surface. She would morph into a vile, indifferent figure, secure in the knowledge that we, her patients, would not be believed if we tried to expose her true nature. Her duplicitous persona derived a twisted satisfaction from this vile charade, reveling in her power to control and manipulate.

During the daytime, I often found a haven in drawing with washable markers and crayons, the only writing instruments I was allowed. Most staff members would warmly supply me with a box of colors and a stack of blank paper to occupy my time. However, when Goldy assumed her duty, my artistic liberty dwindled to a single sheet from a children's coloring book and a lone green marker. Whenever I mustered the courage to ask for the color box, she stubbornly asserted that I was only entitled to what was rationed. Her habitual harassment peaked during the night when she continuously flashed her light on my face. Despite my protests, she persisted, leaving me in a state of sleep deprivation and simmering resentment.

The dietitian in charge of curating our meals was, ironically, morbidly obese herself. She would wheel in our meals on a cart, the food resembling reheated microwave dinners lacking nutritional value. I once erred in requesting a salad. I was greeted by a plastic container filled with white, shredded iceberg lettuce topped off with a single, anemic cherry tomato and a packet of toxic seed oil and high-fructose corn syrup–infused dressing. Our typical meals consisted of highly processed junk food. Instead of real butter, we were handed packets of greasy trans fat loaded with an array of unpronounceable ingredients. The sporadic banana that was provided was either sickeningly green or bruised brown. Infrequent distributions of Nutter Butters or Oreos were the VA's pitiful attempts at raising our morale.

While the facade of care was maintained, the blatant disregard for our overall well-being was striking. Nutrition, sleep, exercise, sunlight, and freedom were sorely missing, making a mockery of this supposed therapeutic refuge. Were these conditions designed to cultivate our health or to make us submissive, lifelong dependents of the pharmaceutical industry? Instead of receiving comprehensive care, we were handed paper ramekins filled with pills. When the staff began introducing additional medications beyond those agreed upon during my consultation with the psychiatrist, I resorted to cheeking them. I decided not to consume more than was necessary, especially given their lack of transparency about these new medications.

The methods employed for our care eerily resembled those used on prisoners of war. Even physically robust military personnel could experience auditory and visual hallucinations after a week of survival training featuring sleep deprivation and confinement. Many of us who ended up at the VA psych ward were already struggling with severe psychosis, wrestling with the most harrowing moments of our lives. The subpar care at the ward felt like a further assault when we were already suffering. I was a prisoner of the ongoing war on mental health in the land of the free.

Conversations with fellow veterans were common during mealtimes, each navigating his unique struggles. Some of them, who had spent time in federal prison, concurred that they were treated better there than at the Battle Creek VA facility. They stated that federal prisons offered superior food, various activities to occupy inmates, and daily opportunities for outdoor exercise. In contrast, the Battle Creek facility was so understaffed that we were lucky to be allowed into the enclosed concrete yard nestled between buildings once a week.

As we played a game of Monopoly, a veteran around my age recounted his experiences with forced electroconvulsive therapy. His detailed account of the excruciating pain troubled me, as did the sight of his visible distress. Another veteran, barely functioning, joined our game, nudging his little wheelbarrow game piece aimlessly around the board. His skull was a patchwork of scars, remnants of multiple invasive brain surgeries. Seeing their enduring anguish and the permanent damage inflicted on them ignited a fury within me. How could this be the treatment of struggling veterans when our patriotic representatives wore American flag lapels and adorned their luxury SUVs with "Support Our Troops" bumper magnets? Falling through society's cracks had laid bare the fragility of its veneer.

I had been voluntarily admitted to the hospital but soon began pleading to return home to my family. This was no place for healing. Despite my incessant pleas, they refused to release me.

My family moved into a nearby dilapidated motel to visit me regularly. Despite its decrepit state, it was the best they could reasonably afford, given the uncertainty of our length of stay in Battle Creek. The grimy motel room was so filthy that Cara had to buy a mop and cleaning supplies and clean the room herself to ensure our toddler didn't get covered in grunge as he crawled around, attempting his first steps.

Yet despite these challenges, they visited me almost every day. Seeing my family was the beacon of hope that kept me going. During these visits, I confided in Cara about the dire conditions at the facility and my urgent desire to return home. My family was not as eager to have me home as I was to leave. My erratic behavior resulted in a prolonged stay at the facility.

I occasionally received sessions with various medical professionals regarding my situation. Dr. Kirby, a psychiatrist, stood out among them with his kindness and compassion. He did everything within his power to provide aid. We would go outside during our meetings to enjoy some fresh air and much-needed sunlight, sitting at a picnic table. As I grew to trust him, I began sharing stories of better times.

I reminisced about my days of mountain biking at the base of Sequoia National Park in Three Rivers, California, while stationed in Lemoore. I shared a vivid memory of unexpectedly riding into a herd of horses towards the end of one such excursion. Startled, they started galloping in the direction I was riding. Soon, I found myself engulfed in a herd of running horses, rushing down the winding trail as if I were one of them. I longed for the freedom I felt in that unforgettable moment, a stark contrast to the confines of the VA asylum. Dr. Kirby appeared sympathetic towards my plight, disturbed by the facility's poor conditions and policies but resolute in doing his best within the constraints. I valued our conversations immensely, though they were rare due to the stretched staffing.

Most of the other doctors, unfortunately, were significantly less compassionate. In one particular session, I was assessed by a senior psychiatrist under the watchful eyes of a group of young medical students scribbling notes. I took the opportunity to criticize them for the facility's failure to provide a healing environment. I questioned how they could expect improvement in our conditions when there was a glaring lack of nutrition, exercise, sunlight, nature, clean water, and sleep, with confinement and constant observation adding to our woes. Most of the fundamentals necessary for healing were replaced with profit-driven, symptom-suppressing pharmaceuticals. This approach did nothing to promote healing and, over time, only served to exacerbate the underlying causes. I expressed my exasperation at what seemed to be a deliberate attempt at teaching these budding professionals to act as minions for the pharmaceutical industry. My pleas, however, fell on deaf ears.

The students, conditioned to stay calm, merely nodded in unison, jotting down notes on their identical clipboards. They assured me, albeit without making eye contact, that they were doing all they could and would reassess my situation for a possible release date in the future. As weeks became what felt like an eternity, my frustration grew exponentially.

In the grip of despair, the thought of escape consumed me. I initiated a covert operation of hoarding warm clothing and packets of snacks, crafting makeshift weapons from wet socks bundled into tied-off tube socks. Covertly, I shared my plan with other veterans, demonstrating how they could create the same crude weapons, subtly instigating a rebellion within the oppressive confines of the facility.

One fateful night, my patience was pushed beyond its limits. In her usual routine, Goldy barged into my room to shine her flashlight directly into my eyes. Despite my pleas for her to stop, she clung to the policy that required this intrusive check every fifteen minutes under the guise of "keeping me safe." Reveling in her authority, she maximized this detrimental policy to its fullest before tormenting more struggling veterans throughout the facility. Worn down by cumulative sleep deprivation, I slumped into my bed.

It seemed as if I had barely shut my eyes when I was abruptly awakened by her flashlight glaring in my face again. Filled with fury, I exploded from my bed and pinned her against the wall. A potent wave of rage coursed through me, inciting a primal urge to rip out her throat. The blood pounded in my ears as I gnashed my teeth and clenched my fists. Her insolence made her blissfully unaware of the danger she was in. Her ignorance of the signs indicating I was on the brink of cracking her skull into the cold, hard tile was astonishing. She was oblivious that she was a breath away from death. The last thread of my remaining humanity held me back from detonating. The overwhelming urge to annihilate her simmered. In a display of my seething anger, I drew my face close to hers, glared into her eyes, took a disdainful sniff, and scorned, "You stink." I stomped back to my bed, too livid to rest.

Fifteen minutes later, I heard the familiar sound of her footsteps resonating down the hallway. Anticipating her intrusive entrance, I hid behind the door, springing on her as she brazenly barged in again. The stench of her hastily applied perfume, an obvious overcompensation for my previous comment, permeated the cramped room. I had reached my breaking point.

Without another word, I brushed past her and pulled the hallway fire alarm, setting in motion the escape plan I had intended for a later time. Another moment spent in Goldy's presence would have undeniably led me to violence. I hoped the alarm would prompt an evacuation, providing the other coherent, desperate souls and me a window for escape. I presumed the more disoriented veterans would be guided back inside, herded like bewildered cattle. Maybe some of us would regain our freedom.

However, the staff, seemingly prepared for such an event, deactivated the alarm and kept us inside. Shortly after, the police arrived. Mike, the head nurse who genuinely cared for the veterans, approached me with a syringe filled with Haldol, a potent antipsychotic medication. He gave me a choice: "We can do this the easy way or the hard way."

Choosing the former, I bent over and made a subtle joke. "Go ahead and stick it in my ass, Mike."

As he injected the Haldol, a sensation akin to insects crawling beneath my skin washed over me. A wave of restlessness seized me, compelling me to run, scream, and claw at my skin to rid myself of the horrible discomfort. This distress only seemed to compound the trauma. After an hour of uncontrolled despair, my body finally succumbed to the FDA-approved injectable hell, and I collapsed. Though the tortuous drug was supposedly given for my well-being, it felt more like a punishment for noncompliance.

I was left drained and weary the following day as they continued administering more oral drugs. I was in a stupor, literally drooling on myself, when a seemingly emotionless lawyer had me scribble on several papers. I could barely comprehend my name, yet I was signing legal documents declaring me mentally defective. I was to be detained indefinitely within the facility. I had been institutionalized.

I was so drugged at that point that I swallowed whatever pills they demanded. My memory washed into a blur. I had become another mindless zombie wandering the halls of the VA nuthouse.

CHAPTER 33

Thankfully, my family's medical knowledge and advocacy eventually released me into their care. If not for their intervention, I might still be trapped in that VA facility, incarcerated for assaulting Goldy—or worse, I could be dead.

Back home, I received a notice stating that my concealed carry license had been revoked. The documents I had signed while heavily sedated had legally declared me permanently mentally defective. I had voluntarily checked into the VA psychiatric hospital to receive medical treatment for injuries I had sustained during my honorable military service. In return, I had been forcibly drugged, detained, tormented, and stripped of my inalienable civil liberties. I am no longer legally allowed to purchase a firearm. My name was entered into the Law Enforcement Information Network, or LEIN. If the police pull me over, my name will appear in their database as if I have committed a crime.

*　　　*　　　*

With newfound freedom from my confining circumstances, I could finally spend time outdoors with my son. Regrettably, part of his tender years had been tarnished by visits to his father in a mental institution. He had grown from an unsteady toddler to a speedy little boy who could run, jump, and climb. As for me, I struggled with everyday tasks as simple as washing dishes.

Trapped in the depths of despair, I felt estranged from my son, unable to experience any semblance of love or joy. When he would innocently approach me, asking if we could play, he was met with his emotionally detached, over-medicated, grumbling father telling him to go away. In my anguished state, I distanced myself from everyone who showed me care and affection. I felt like a dying old dog, yearning to wander off into the solitude of the woods to meet its end alone.

Despite the relentless side effects, the VA psychiatrist continued to prescribe quetiapine. He was a kind man who truly wanted to help struggling veterans, but his toolbox only contained one broken tool: psychotropic medications. The VA psychiatrist repeatedly told me this was how my life would be. According to him and all the professionals I had access to through the VA, the best treatment was to continue taking my prescription meds for the rest of my life. There was no other option. I had complied with their advice, but there had to be a different approach to healing. While thankful for the financial support provided by the VA as part of my medical retirement, I needed to find a new option for my recovery.

My longtime friend and creator of my nickname "Scrappy," Matt, gave me a book by Rich Roll called *Finding Ultra*. The side effects from the drugs and the unresolved brain injury often made it nearly impossible for me to remember even a paragraph at a time. Some days, I couldn't even remember a complete sentence. It took me months of slow rereading to get through the book, but I retained some helpful advice.

In *Finding Ultra*, Roll discusses how he transformed from an overweight, alcohol-dependent corporate attorney into an ultra-endurance athlete through hearty plant-based meals and regular exercise. I started to incorporate some of his dietary and exercise recommendations alongside the venison I would harvest with my crossbow each autumn.

With a glimmer of hope spurred by the slight health improvements I experienced through small meal changes, I started to learn more about nutrition. Still dealing with cognitive deficits and side effects, I clumsily read *In Defense of Food* by Michael Pollan. I had considered myself a healthy eater until then, but I quickly gained a new understanding of just how much artificial junk is present in most food in the United States.

Many of the ingredients used in the United States are illegal for food in most other developed countries. The US industrial food industry has persistently bolstered its profits by replacing increasingly more real ingredients with harmful artificial fillers, flavors, and colors. Almost everything in the grocery store has devolved into ultra-processed junk over the past few decades, beyond just desserts and snacks.

Just by examining the ingredients of a simple peanut butter and jelly sandwich, one can become acutely aware of the number of undesirable substances in our food. Pick up a conventional loaf of bread, and you'll find a long list of unpronounceable ingredients not found in a homemade loaf. Conventionally grown modern wheat has devolved into an inflammatory substance loaded with toxic herbicides. Most commercial peanut butter is filled with harmful hydrogenated oils, and the standard jelly is packed with high fructose corn syrup and artificial colors. You can find natural, unprocessed foods if you're lucky to live near a health food store. However, this is a luxury that many Americans don't have access to.

Even fruits and vegetables have considerably declined in nutritional value. Nowadays, you'd have to eat five apples to get the same nutrients that a single apple grown in the 1950s would have provided. This is partly due to the overworked, nutrient-depleted, fertilizer-dependent soils in which most American produce is grown.

Conventional produce also contains the harmful substance glyphosate, the active ingredient in the widely used herbicide Roundup. Glyphosate wreaks havoc on our digestive systems and the micronutrients in the soil that are vital for our bodies' healthy functions. Yes, it kills unwanted weeds, but it destroys all life, including our gut microbiome, which is crucial to our overall health.

Developed initially as a military tank cleaner, glyphosate's destructive potential was noticed when soldiers saw the grass dying around their freshly cleaned equipment. Despite the well-known harmful effects on humans and the environment, they continue to manufacture and sell this highly profitable toxin. Regulatory agencies consistently fail to protect us from toxic substances like glyphosate, so we must protect ourselves. I prefer my food without tank cleaner.

Joel Salatin, a regenerative farmer, author, and speaker from Polyface Farm, provides abundant information on how our food system has deteriorated. He also proposes practical solutions despite industry resistance and red tape. The United States Department of Agriculture (USDA), tasked with protecting the public from harmful practices, has become a captive agency of the heavily subsidized industry it's supposed to regulate. Instead of safeguarding the people, the USDA has become a tool for the most prominent players in the industry to create obstacles for small regenerative farmers trying to offer healthier alternatives.

Unhealthy, nutrient-poor foods remain cheap and accessible due to government subsidies, while healthier options are suppressed by the same corporations benefiting from keeping the established corrupt system broken. The reason these junk foods are so cheap is mainly that taxpayers' money subsidizes them. Consequently, most people consume food that contributes to more costly health problems, such as obesity, diabetes, heart disease, and mental health complications. Combine this with polluted drinking water, declining air quality, excessive alcohol consumption, sleep-deprived lifestyles, and the ever-increasing array of toxins we're exposed to every day, and it's not hard to see why so many people suffer from chronic illnesses.

Despite the discomfort of exercising with quetiapine in my system, I utilized the mountain bike trails near my house. Ripping down the winding single-track trails and dodging trees helped me focus on the present rather than dwelling in the past or fretting about the future. Despite the medication's warning to avoid exercise due to a risk of impaired body temperature regulation and possible heat stroke, I continued to push myself physically. While my physical injuries limited me to a fraction of my former capabilities, the benefits seemed worthwhile.

CHAPTER 34

With her unwavering optimism, Cara had faced numerous adversities, but my recent traumatic hospitalization had irrevocably altered something within me. I was a changed man, no longer the person she had fallen in love with. A chasm began to form between us, slowly but steadily expanding. My all-consuming depression was snuffing out any glimmers of hope I would ever recover or improve, deepening our divide further.

As the years passed, I felt like I had trapped my wife in a cage. I could sense her resentment growing, and our discussions of divorce became more frequent as we sought a reasonable path forward.

My misadventures with pharmaceutical-based treatments continued until I stumbled upon Michael Pollan's book *How to Change Your Mind*, which details the benefits of psychedelics for treating mental illness. On days when my mental faculties allowed, I read through the book and recognized that psychedelic therapy might be my way forward.

With the help of a skilled guide, I participated in a psilocybin mushroom ceremony despite my family's doubts and persistent warnings against pursuing this type of alternative treatment. Though the psychedelic psilocybin didn't solve all my problems instantly, it did offer a new path. Using Michael Pollan's analogy, it felt like fresh snowfall had smoothed over the rutted emotional landscape of my life. With the ruts of anger, depression, and past trauma covered, I could carve a new path. I began to see the pattern of my treatment with quetiapine for what it was: an insane cycle. Despite being repeatedly portrayed as my only hope, I noticed that as my dose increased, my condition worsened. Against the advice of my psychiatrist and family, I decided to wean myself off quetiapine.

People have been conditioned to believe that withdrawing from psychotropic medication can lead to a disaster. Undoubtedly, once these drugs have gripped someone, their absence can result in psychosis. However, I was caught in a state of being that was neither living nor dying, existing as a depressed, emotionless husk. I had to try something. Over several months, I slowly lowered my dosage of quetiapine despite the swirling worries within me. Concurrently, I laid a foundation for healthier lifestyle habits to give my body the best chance to adjust to this change.

As I steadily decreased my nightly dose over months, my battle with insomnia raged on, but eventually, I could catch a few hours of sleep each night unassisted. When I felt myself slipping back into paranoia and hypervigilance, I would take just enough quetiapine to ensure at least a sip of sleep. After several grueling months, I finally freed myself from the shackles of psychotropic medications.

Without the medication dulling my senses and numbing my spirit, I began to feel a gradual resurgence in my health. It was subtle at first, but just enough for Cara and me to take a leap of faith and welcome another child into our lives. The birth of our beautiful, fiery daughter was a turning point. Although I still struggled to reconnect with my emotions fully, something profound stirred within me each time I held my children. Their warmth, innocence, and unconditional love began to awaken a part of me that had long been dormant. It was as if their light was slowly coaxing my soul back to life, one heartbeat at a time.

I sought to join a groundbreaking psychedelic healing program facilitated by Veterans Exploring Treatment Solutions (VETS). This nonprofit organization, founded by former Navy SEAL Marcus Capone and his wife, Amber, is at the forefront of efforts to broaden access to these medicinal treatments for veterans nationwide. Vet Solutions provides grants to veterans grappling with post-traumatic stress and traumatic brain injury, collectively becoming referred to as operator syndrome, facilitating their access to legal psychedelic therapies abroad.

As VETS founder Marcus Capone points out, it's a disheartening irony that America's most devoted veterans must travel to foreign lands to heal wounds incurred while fighting for the freedoms their homeland proudly proclaims. Obsolete and restrictive policies, remnants of the catastrophically failed war on drugs, obstruct the usage of transformative indigenous medicines. These substances have been inappropriately classified in the same Schedule I category as highly addictive and easily abused substances with no legitimate medical benefits. This fear is a holdover from the cultural wars of past generations. Hopefully, the fear will fade as the surge of injured veterans healing from indigenous medicines continues to grow.

Despite the undeniable success and surging demand for the Vet Solutions program, my application was passed over. The program's entry criteria prioritize Special Forces personnel with combat experience, a category I did not belong to. Marcus and Amber's situation mirrors that of *Schindler's List*—they sincerely wished to assist everyone but were constrained by the available resources and reliant on donations.

CHAPTER 35

A glimmer of hope arrived late one night, weeks later, in an email from VETS introducing me to another nonprofit, the Warrior Angels Foundation (WAF). This organization, run by former Green Beret Andrew Marr and his brother Adam, a former US Army Apache helicopter pilot, was devoted to a similar cause. Andrew and Adam co-authored the best-selling book *Tales from the Blast Factory*, which provided a detailed account of Andrew's struggles with brain injury and PTSD and his journey toward finding effective medical treatment after years of adversity. Through the guidance of Dr. Mark Gordon, Andrew discovered a successful treatment approach that obviated the need for debilitating psychotropic medications. Their book was adapted into a powerful documentary, *Quiet Explosions*. Reading their book and watching the documentary encouraged me to find practical strategies for brain repair and managing TBI/PTS symptoms.

WAF was organizing an event based on a challenge conceived by the "hardest man alive," former Navy SEAL David Goggins: the Goggins 4x4x48 Challenge. The challenge involved running four miles every four hours for forty-eight straight hours. I shared a brief account of my story on WAF's fundraising page for the event. Having no presence on social media at the time, I sent the fundraiser link to friends and family via text, not expecting much. It was the first time I shared

Recording one of my first podcast episodes with former combat veteran turned fearless veteran advocate Kelsi Sheren at the Warrior Angels Foundation 4x4x48 Challenge. Kelsi's encouragement to speak openly about my struggles inspired me to write this book.

my experiences with the VA publicly. Feeling alone and broken, I thought that no one cared about me. But I couldn't have been more wrong. The fundraising page quickly garnered thousands of dollars in donations, with friends, family, and strangers demonstrating overwhelming support for my recovery and that of other veterans.

A few days later, my phone rang, and on the other end was Adam Marr from WAF. He invited me to Texas for the 4x4x48 Challenge. Despite the nerve damage and atrophy in my left foot that resulted in a limp, I was excited to participate. I felt a strong pull to go, pushing my concerns aside.

When I arrived in Texas, I was warmly welcomed at the airport with a bear hug from the massive Andrew Marr. He brought me to their secluded ranch, where I was immediately embraced by a community of veterans all walking similar paths to recovery from PTS and TBI. The participants included SEALs, Green Berets, Rangers, US Marines, MARSOC Raiders, various tier-one operators, and some individuals whose service details remained classified. We were even joined by former Secretary of Defense Lieutenant General Christopher Miller, who had served as a Green Beret before becoming SECDEF. He recognized the current approach to helping veterans suffering from TBI/PTS was unacceptable. Despite our service-related injuries having various origins, it was clear we all suffered from brain injuries. Overmedicated and with an excessive focus on our PTSD diagnoses, we shared similar experiences. There, I was introduced to many highly effective modalities for healing the brain and symptoms commonly associated with PTS—modalities many of these incredible warriors had already successfully employed.

Chief Phil Lane Jr. of the Ihanktonwan Dakota and Chickasaw Nations initiated the event by passing Crazy Horse's renowned pipe, and then the run commenced. By my side was Kelsi Sheren, a passionate, petite woman who served as a combat veteran in the Canadian Forces and later started a successful company called Brass and Unity. We shared stories throughout the first leg, with me recounting my ejection experience. She showed great interest in my tale and proposed an interview for her *Brass and Unity* podcast. I was humbled to be part of this group alongside these elite soldiers who had braved so much in combat. It was profoundly therapeutic to share my traumas openly with individuals who truly understood the trials of mental health struggles.

With every leg of the run, I met more veterans who had experienced similar trials and mismanagement in their medical treatment. The confirmation that I was on the right path felt deeply reassuring. Despite my family's and psychiatrist's disagreement, I wasn't insane to think the medications had exacerbated my condition. I discovered that psychotropic drugs harm around 90 percent of the patients they're prescribed to, including every veteran I talked to at the event.

Sixteen miles in, my atrophied left foot throbbed with pain, and shin splints further complicated the run. US Army Special Forces veteran and ultra-endurance athlete Vance McMurry came to my aid. Vance cofounded AutoTelic Performance Solutions, a company specializing in optimizing human performance. He and his business partner, former Green Beret Harold Hill, who served in the US Army Special Forces for twenty-six years, offered their assistance. Although I was unaware of these men's legendary status in their field, they treated me like one of their own.

Vance introduced me to a small electrical device called the NeuX. As he connected it to my shins, it sent small pulses of electricity through my muscles, causing repeated contractions. It reminded me of a TENS unit, often used for pain management, but this device used a specialized combination of frequencies comprised of alternating pulsed AC and DC currents. After a ten-minute session with the NeuX, my shin splints dissipated. Vance offered advice on how to prevent ankle collapse and consequential pain by adjusting the alignment of my toes as fatigue set in. Heeding his advice, I discovered I felt stronger as the run persisted.

Each visit to Harold and Vance's aid station throughout the event introduced me to healing resources that would benefit me and my family. Vance applied the NeuX pads to my neck and lower back, allowing a gentle current to flow through my body, inducing a state of calm and clarity—the so-called "flow state." Vance and Harold explored the use of this device In training and operations for elite military units and SWAT teams, finding significant improvements in performance under high-stress scenarios. Such cutting-edge technology could prove invaluable for military pilots. However, despite their potential, this and other effective healing modalities were unavailable through VA hospitals or TRICARE insurance.

The Warrior Angels Foundation event opened my eyes to a world of healing that mainstream medicine ignores or suppresses mainly because these modalities threaten the business model employed by the pharmaceutical and insurance industries currently controlling health care. Big pharma and the insurance industry usually dismiss anything that isn't a lifetime pill prescription. They are notorious for buying out promising technologies and scrapping them or using their sway over the FDA to outlaw them, regardless of their safety or effectiveness. These practices continue today.

During the two transformational days of endurance and self-discovery, I was invited into a circle of Native Americans partaking in a peyote ceremony. Late into the night, my body thrumming from the over thirty miles already ground into my muscles, I ducked into their teepee. I scooped a spoonful of the bitter cactus concoction with a tea chaser to wash it down. We sat in a circle, the Natives stoking the heart of the teepee with long timbers. The heat surged, the chant rose, and the drums reverberated against my ribcage. They excused us, mid-ceremony, to complete another four-mile leg in the darkness.

Experiencing profound healing at the Warrior Angels Foundation
Challenge Run through an indigenous ceremony, combined with
reconnecting to my community and purpose.

Racing through the woods, my senses were dialed up to eleven, my body fresh despite the miles behind me. I was running alongside these veterans, sharing tales of our experience, overmedicated and abandoned. This leg seemed to melt away beneath our feet, time and distance flowing pleasantly. When I returned to camp, the world was asleep. A couple of diehards and I crashed the ongoing peyote ceremony in the teepee.

Inside those glowing walls, the others were lost in the depths of the ceremony. The heat was a slap in the face; the drumming and chanting were a symphony hammering my eardrums. With a larger helping of the peyote paste, I was lost in the swirl of sound, heat, and indigenous medicine. When I came up for air, the late-night leg was already history. My exit was abrupt, embarrassment nipping at my heels as I ran out of the ceremony. The starting line was a ghost town, volunteers gone, runners back in their tents. I found a lone volunteer, a former US Army Ranger, and told him I was running the leg solo. He grinned, nodded, and sent me off into the night alone.

The dying glimmers of vehicle lights disappeared behind me as I killed my headlamp, plunging into the abyss of night. Ahead, there was an old two-track trail washed out and decorated with potholes and jutting rocks, a perfect recipe for a twisted ankle or worse. But the peyote had sharpened my senses, becoming a guide through the darkness. Initially, I was blind to the world; the night was pitch-black, the new moon obscured by a thick layer of broken clouds. Despite the murk, I eased into a slow jog, my eyes taking their sweet time adjusting to the dark.

Soon enough, I spotted openings in the tree line above me, tiny windows directing me through the winding hills. Stars began to show their faces as the clouds parted, twinkling a silent encouragement. It was a moment of pure presence; my senses synchronized with the universe surrounding me. A fleeting thought crossed my mind of how advantageous peyote could be during night flight ops around the boat. I was alert, clearheaded, and hyperaware, my senses on overdrive.

A heart rate–displaying watch adorned my wrist, a constant companion throughout the event. Typically, I'd steal glances at it to ensure I was under 140 beats per minute, keeping me in the sweet spot of zone 2 heart rate and maximizing my endurance. I was so attuned to my body that I didn't need the digital reassurance. I knew exactly where my heart rate was; the few times I cross-checked out of curiosity, it was bang on 140.

The trail was a roller coaster of ups and downs. I'd habitually walked uphill sections to conserve my energy, but I couldn't distinguish the slopes from the flats in the shroud of darkness. Yet I felt like I was floating, my legs moving effortlessly over the rugged terrain. My pace was faster, my heart rate was steady, and without the sight of impending hills, I saved the mental energy that usually went into anticipation. It made me ponder the energy we squander on worries and what-ifs. Alone on that dark trail, under the watchful eyes of the stars, I found my freedom.

Returning to camp, a smattering of high fives from the few volunteers who had waited up for me, my mind was alive with thoughts and feelings. Nestled in my sleeping bag, eyes tracing the outlines of constellations, I was a spark in the vast universe.

*   *   *

The pre-dawn quiet was shattered by the music blaring from a massive speaker stationed in the open field where we were camping. I hadn't managed more than a few hours of sleep since the beginning of the event two days prior, but my body was buzzing with an inexplicable energy. I took on the final legs of the event with enthusiasm, feeling nothing of the soreness or fatigue that should have settled in by then. It was as though the Native Comanche spirits that once occupied these woods were spurring me on, imbuing me with a weightless euphoria.

Sprinting the final miles, I crossed the finish line, my heart brimming with a love so overwhelming it felt like I might burst. That day, the energy was something out of a dream, an incredibly special beacon in the archives of my memory.

The event came to a poignant close, with the Natives guiding us through a staking ceremony. We gathered around, forming a large circle as the elders began their speeches about healing. Given the historical context between the US military and these Natives' forefathers, the sheer volume of love directed toward us was overwhelming. It was a sight to behold, these tattooed, muscle-bound warriors all reduced to tears. Unabashedly, I let my tears of joy flow.

The elders invited us to connect with an old tree standing solitarily in the pasture, to place our intentions with it. I hung back, waiting for the crowd to dwindle before approaching. The moment I put my hand and forehead against the bark of the tree, a surge of energy coursed through me, accompanied by a blinding flash of white light. In that split second, whatever spirit or entity communicating through that tree seemed to understand me, welcoming me to partake in this peaceful revolution as a brother.

Without a single word exchanged, I was shown a vision of my purpose. I was meant to do incredible things in life, to be a beacon of healing, and this moment of epiphany marked the beginning of my mission to aid in others' healing, starting with sharing my own story. All my suffering had been for a purpose. That day, we all became torchbearers of hope for the world. I felt like I had been inducted into the Rebel Alliance. I was a fucking Jedi.

CHAPTER 36

Coming back from Texas, I was effervescent with newfound hope. Former Green Beret Andrew Marr's wise guidance echoed in my head: *Be the captain of your own ship*. After a grueling barrage of gale-force headwinds, tumultuous storms, and being told that healing was a fairy tale, I felt like I had finally drifted upon a course leading me back to myself. It was time to man the helm.

When I arrived home, radiating optimism, it became painfully clear that my wife was skeptical. Years of bearing witness to my emotional turmoil had formed a protective shell around her; she had ceased trusting me as a self-preservation mechanism. Cara, my steadfast rock throughout these years, was emotionally worn. The trauma had carved deep grooves in her, pushing a seemingly unbridgeable gap between us. Her skepticism seemed to swallow most of the light I had returned home with. This beautiful woman, who had endured so much and had repeatedly been refused help by the VA caregiver program, needed my consistent support now. It was time to sail our relationship out of the darkness together, but we had to avoid the treacherous rocks hiding beneath the surface.

We found ourselves trapped in a vicious, self-perpetuating cycle that seemed impossible to break. Whenever one of us attempted to be vulnerable and open up, the other would instinctively put up walls, retreating into a protective shell. It was as if our individual traumas acted as triggers, setting off alarms that kept us in a constant state of defense. Any attempt at meaningful communication would quickly disintegrate; what started as an effort to connect would escalate into a spat within seconds, often over the most trivial things.

The emotional wounds from our pasts acted like an invisible force field between us. Whenever I would try to share my fears or insecurities, Cara would sense my hesitation and, in turn, withdraw. The moment she would attempt to reach out, I would find myself reacting from a place of pain, raising my defenses even higher. Each of us felt abandoned by the other, which only reinforced our need to protect ourselves. This cycle of retreat and resistance created a barrier that grew thicker and more impenetrable with every argument.

We were both desperate to be understood, but neither of us felt safe enough to drop our guard completely. It was as if our past traumas were battling each other, with neither willing to surrender or acknowledge the other's pain. The walls we had built to shield ourselves from hurt ended up being the very things that kept us isolated, unable to truly connect with the person standing right in front of us.

Over time, the cycle wore us down. The more we tried to communicate, the more we seemed to push each other away, and the harder it became to find our way back to the love we once shared. It was as if our relationship had become a battlefield, each of us armed with the weapons of our past, striking out before the other could strike first. Our marriage had become a war zone, and the casualties were the trust, intimacy, and connection we once had.

Unable to make progress on our own, we contacted the Vet Center, an extension of the VA, for couples counseling. We hoped it would provide support amid our trials or at least a mediator to referee. However, the outcome was a brutal blow from the institution that was supposed to be on our side.

After attending a few sessions, Cara and I saw some incremental improvements in our relationship, though we had a long way to go. During one of my absences, Cara attended a one-on-one session. Prompted by a question about her trust issues, she bravely shared the harrowing memory of me, in a state of psychosis, with a shoelace around our son's neck from years ago when she was getting ready to rush me to the emergency room.

Despite the incident being a distant memory with no harm done to our son, the therapist, without any forewarning, reported us to Child Protective Services (CPS). During my absence, CPS arrived at our home, interrogated Cara, and intruded into our personal spaces. Cara held onto this traumatic incident until I returned home a few days later. As she recounted the experience, a torrent of fury swept over me. The idea that we could lose our children simply because we sought counseling to strengthen our relationship was another heartrending betrayal.

CPS informed us that they would return to interview me. The suspense over the potential removal of our children was unbearable. Sleep eluded me the entire week as I braced for CPS's return. Dark thoughts of violent confrontations flitted through my mind as I stewed in my anger. No way were they going to abduct my children.

When the CPS agent arrived, she cautiously sat down to question me. My rage seethed just beneath the surface. As she started probing, my son climbed into my lap, hugged me tightly, and told me, "Daddy, I love you." His innocent act of affection seemed to jolt the agent into realizing the baselessness of her presence, and she promptly left. If my warmhearted son hadn't instinctively comforted me at that moment, there's no telling what further damage could have been done to our family.

That was the last time we attended couples counseling through the Vet Center—yet another broken support system for veterans.

Through the recommendation of the same healer who had guided my transformative psilocybin journey, Cara and I discovered an alternative couples counseling option. This married couple specialized in holistic and spiritual approaches to therapy. Although their services weren't covered by insurance and required us to pay out of pocket, we quickly realized that investing in this process was far more valuable than the cost of a potential divorce.

The counselors combined elements of traditional couples therapy with more spiritual and metaphysical practices. They helped us address our communication gaps, teaching us how to listen and understand one another again truly. Their approach was different from anything we had tried before, encouraging us to explore not only our individual wounds but also how our energies interacted and impacted the relationship. We engaged in exercises that pushed us to be vulnerable, honest, and present—qualities that had been lost in the chaos of my trauma and recovery.

As our sessions progressed, Cara and I began to feel a reconnection that went deeper than anything we had experienced in our relationship up to that point. The culmination of our counseling journey was a psilocybin and cacao ceremony led by the counseling couple, where Cara and I embarked on a shared journey of healing and introspection. As the psilocybin opened our minds and the warm cacao filled our hearts, we confronted the pain, fears, and insecurities that had driven us apart.

Our son captured this moment of reconnection between Cara and me in Huntington Beach shortly after I completed the thirty-mile paddle from Catalina Island to the California coast with OpenWater, becoming an official Rusty Anchor.

In that sacred space, we saw each other clearly—our vulnerabilities, strengths, and love buried beneath years of struggle. The ceremony became a powerful catalyst for healing, allowing us to rebuild our relationship on a foundation of mutual understanding, acceptance, and unconditional love. It was the moment we realized that despite everything we had been through, we were still capable of finding our way back to each other.

Enjoying the California coast with my family.

As our conversations gradually became more open and our defenses began to fall, not only did we start to reconnect, but the entire atmosphere of our home shifted as well. Our children sensed the positive change and began to flourish, responding to our renewed harmony. With Mom and Dad finally back on the same team, our house genuinely transformed into a home filled with laughter, love, and understanding. It wasn't a quick fix, but we rebuilt our foundation step by step, stronger and more resilient than before and ready to face whatever life would throw at us next.

CHAPTER 37

Having met Jesse Gould, the founder of the Heroic Hearts Project, at the Challenge event a few months prior, I was invited to the breathtaking Soltara Healing Center, La Medicina, in Tarapoto, Peru. I plunged into three nights of potent ayahuasca ceremonies with seven other veterans under the watchful eyes of two indigenous Shipibo shamans hailing from the Amazon. It was like a surgical intervention for our souls, nestled within the emerald-green blanket of the rainforest.

Profound healing in the Amazon rainforest near Tarapoto, Peru, during a week of intense indigenous ceremony with the Shipibo.

Our first night with the medicine was primarily introductory. Ayahuasca, a potent brew made from the bark of the winding black ayahuasca vine and chacruna (a common bush in the rainforest), simmered over a fire in a cauldron for eight hours. I braced myself for the journey ahead after downing a shot glass of the bitter concoction while nursing hand-rolled mapacho tobacco in the circle of my fellow voyagers.

An hour into the wait, I barely felt anything until one of the Shipibo shamans approached me. As soon as he started to chant the icaro, spiritual energy seemed to infuse into me. I plunged headfirst into a whirlpool of fractal patterns and spiraling hallucinations. It felt like the bite of a venomous snake: nauseating and weakening but, in a weird twist, comforting. It was as if I was in the belly of a gigantic snake, being digested and infused by its unpleasant yet nurturing venom. The jungle's nocturnal symphony of insects and amphibians seemed to amplify and guide my hallucinations.

After a few hours, a shaman blew ceremonial perfume toward me, and the droplets splattering on my skin erupted into spirals of red and white, reminiscent of peppermint swirls. I promptly found myself purging into my bucket—a reaction seen as a compliment by the Shipibo. I sensed that ayahuasca was merely showing me a glimpse of its capabilities and that the real journey was yet to unfold.

Once the first night ceremony wrapped up, I managed to stumble back to my room, purging one last time before bed. As I did, I witnessed a dark, twisted, muscular entity being expelled from me and dissolving into the toilet bowl. It felt like a long-trapped malevolent force within me had finally vacated. With nausea gone, I managed to lie down, but sleep evaded me as my mind teemed with thoughts, my gaze fixed on the serene sunrise.

The next day was spent relishing the freshest produce I had ever tasted. The rainforest soil, rich with nutrients, had endowed the plants with an unmatched tenderness and natural flavor that required no dressing. Though smaller than my usual portion, the satisfying nutrient-dense meals satiated me. Midday, we were bathed in a fragrant flower bath by the Shipibo, a soothing ritual that seemed to strengthen our bond. As we ventured through the dense jungle, we felt like old comrades, our collective experience already forging a deep connection between us.

As sunset again draped the rainforest in darkness, we commenced the ceremony for the second night. I imbibed the same quantity of ayahuasca as the previous night. Instead of the nausea that followed the first time, I fell into an immersive silence, broken only by the gentle glow of mapacho cigarettes and the ambient hum of the jungle. Suddenly, the room began to spin, its rhythm seeming to flow like water in a counterclockwise swirl above me, leading me into a world hidden in the darkest corners of my psyche.

I descended into an abyss of horror, filled with screams of terror and retching sounds. I felt the presence of others being tormented alongside me, the rancid smell of vomit and excrement choking my senses. It was as if I was chained in a boundless, pitch-black void, a purgatory that squeezed me tighter the more I struggled. I was separated from my physical form, adrift in a timeless void.

Over the years, my inner child had been fortified behind layers of protective walls, but in doing so, I had inadvertently incarcerated myself within a labyrinth of agonizing pain. That night, I embarked on a hazardous journey deep into the depths of this labyrinth, seeking to liberate my soul. It was an uphill battle, but the Shipibo shamans guided me through with their ethereal icaros. After what felt like an eternity of being trapped and spiraling into madness, I succumbed, curling into a fetal position at the heart of my personal hell. Complete surrender was the only option.

The moment I relinquished control, my soul broke free. The labyrinthine walls crumbled away as the rage within me, my inner firestone, erupted into a brilliant starlight. My spirit ascended from the abyss, taking on various forms: insects, frogs, humans, and other organisms. I lived an entire lifetime as an ancient Amazonian tree, watching generations of human civilization rise and fall in what felt like a single breath.

My perspective expanded further, transforming into the spirit of Earth, then the sun, followed by the Milky Way galaxy, until I embodied the entire universe. What transpired in a few hours felt like an endless journey through eons. The shackles of time didn't exist in this spiritual realm. Every breath was like a life cycle, with new life emerging and dying with each inhale and exhale.

This extraordinary journey taught me the essence of yin and yang, the duality of light and dark, and their inherent unity. I was shown a glimpse of divinity's infiniteness tailored to my human mind's limited understanding and sensory capacity. I sensed the interconnectedness of everything in the universe, hinting at a profound link between all beings that transcends the basic five human senses.

That third eye of mine wasn't just ajar now; it was swung wide open, a stargate into the interlaced energy of the cosmos, its dimensions, its universe, its multiverse—oneness. Ayahuasca played the role of the key master, steering me into a semi-lucid, dreamlike sphere of reality where the reins of existence were mine. I had the power to be anything and everything, the freedom to traverse anywhere and everywhere. Limitations were only an archaic echo. I discovered the divine within me, the same divinity dwelling within all of us.

The odyssey through my consciousness that night held a depth and breadth that mere human language falls short of expressing. As I began retracing my steps to our plane of reality, a cosmic pit stop presented itself. There, in a sanctum of spirits, I took my seat. Each entity witnessed the dawn of time and told tales of their journeys. The future was not a mystery here, for they, too, speculated the path it was to take. No words were spoken; our interaction was a symphony of resonations and sound waves, a music only spirit could comprehend. I understood and reckoned those with me were the souls of the veterans who accompanied me that night.

Back in my terrestrial vessel, back in our collective consciousness known as reality, I woke up to the tranquility that permeated the room. The ceremony had concluded, leaving traces of an evening of intense transformations. Purging was commonplace that night in various forms, from vomiting to defecating, sweating to crying, shaking to even laughing. Each form of purge cleared trapped energy and emotions from our souls, allowing the medicine to work even deeper. The retreat's wise keeper chuckled at these displays of bodily surrender, going so far as to label a simultaneous act of vomiting and defecating a "double platinum." Judging by the room's state, it was clear someone had scored a quadruple platinum.

Finally able to find my feet, I slowly descended the winding path of stone stairs toward a clearing in the jungle's embrace. A circular patch of grass with a round concrete platform at its heart beckoned. As I approached it, an insect the size of a hummingbird startled me, thrashing into my hair before buzzing back into the night. I found my place in the circle, craning my neck to drink in the cosmic spectacle overhead.

Absent of light pollution and with the medicine enhancing my senses, the stars shone with a vibrancy I had never experienced before. It was as if I stood at the edge of our solar system, the universe around me caressing me with its cosmic dance. Each star was a radiant burst from my being, connecting me to every pinprick of light in the sky.

On the concluding night, my consciousness was given free rein again. I ventured where my spirit willed, strolling down memory lane and visiting loved ones. I dove into my parent's hearts, feeling their despair and helplessness when I was trapped in a coma following my ejection, a shadow between life and death. The anguish of potentially losing a child made me weep, but it was a tender moment of connection with them, a shared experience that transcended time.

Next, I ventured to my sleeping wife and children, showering them with invisible caresses, a spectral visitor in the night. Then, a strange sensation flooded me—I was merging with a black jaguar. I could feel its power coursing through my being, the strength of the large feline, as I stretched out my paws and clawed into a tree, releasing the tension in my sore shoulder and back. The jaguar became my healer, showing me the path to recovery after injury. For the rest of the ceremony, my body moved through yoga postures. The strength and grace of the jaguar spirit and mine merged as one.

As dawn broke the following day, we gathered in a fellowship like the Knights of the Round Table, recounting our experiences. The retreat's owner, a seasoned traveler in the realm of ayahuasca, emanated wisdom. Before we set off on our individual journeys, he shared a profound thought that resonated with me: "We are spiritual beings having a human experience." The ayahuasca and the Shipibo guides were my spiritual medics, repairing the fractures in my soul.

Since my Peruvian odyssey, life has flowed more smoothly, each moment a breath, a cycle of existence. No longer am I simply surviving; I'm relearning to thrive. Like a phoenix, I was revived from the ashes, emboldened by my struggles and renewed with a fiery determination to persevere.

CHAPTER 38

My healing journey started with an extensive blood panel. Without this detailed snapshot of my physiology, doctors could be operating blind. However, insurance restrictions often limit the use of these crucial diagnostic tools. Luckily, I managed to get a comprehensive blood panel done, and just as important, I had a doctor who understood how to interpret the results accurately.

The community I had discovered through the Warrior Angels Foundation had become an invaluable lifeline. They introduced me to Dr. Michael Lewis, a highly respected physician and the author of *When Brains Collide*. His book detailed the incredible healing potential of high-quality omega-3 fatty acids. Working up to a dose of 3,000 milligrams per day, I started to see how this could help heal my brain. The high-quality fatty acids helped reduce inflammation and supplied my brain with the healthy fats needed for recovery.

Dr. Lewis explained that several of my biomarkers were abnormal compared to healthy standards. He shed light on the hormonal imbalances that often follow brain injury and how these can contribute to emotional instability, depression, sleep disorders, memory issues, focus problems, and other conditions. It became clear that much of what I struggled with could be traced back to these imbalances. With this knowledge, I adhered to my nutraceutical supplementation and addressed these imbalances under Dr. Lewis's guidance and with the support of the Warrior Angels Foundation.

The Warrior Angels Foundation also connected me with Dr. Mark Gordon, an esteemed expert in brain injury recovery. He has made multiple appearances on the podcast *The Joe Rogan Experience* alongside Andrew Marr. Doc Gordon explained our brain's fragility and the potential cumulative damage from even mundane knocks, but he also stressed the resilience of the human brain and its remarkable ability to recover when given the right conditions.

*   *   *

I also connected with Defenders of Freedom, a charitable organization that supports veterans through unconventional TBI treatments. Intrigued by my tale, the founder of Defenders of Freedom, Donna Cranston, extended an invitation for two weeks of therapy at Resiliency Brain Health in Dallas. Before setting foot in Texas, I subjected myself to the most comprehensive blood panel I'd ever taken. By the time I arrived, Dr. Scharlene Gaudet had acquired a more profound understanding of my physiology than I'd ever known.

Day one at the clinic was all about assessments. "Doc G," as most call her, spent hours evaluating my neural dysfunctions through various hands-on tests. Balance checks and cognitive exams, including memory and attention assessments, were put under her meticulous eye. She mapped my cerebral landscape using a cutting-edge transcranial magnetic stimulation (TMS) instrument. From the plethora of tests, it was determined that the right side of my brain had been severely impacted by trauma in the ejection.

Doc G explained that a brain injury resembled someone recklessly yanking out all the RCA cables from a sophisticated sound studio mixer. As the brain embarks on its healing journey, the "cables" get plugged back in, albeit often not into their original sockets. Using the magnetic impulses of the TMS, she stimulated a part of my brain that should've controlled a finger; instead, my leg experienced a peculiar tingling sensation. Anomalies of this sort repeatedly emerged throughout the detailed examination, with abnormal eye movement being another pointer to my cerebral dysfunction. By the end of the assessments, it was painfully clear that I was grappling with multiple issues. It casts a shadow of doubt over the VA neurologist's paltry 10 percent TBI rating, questioning their competence, their integrity, or possibly both.

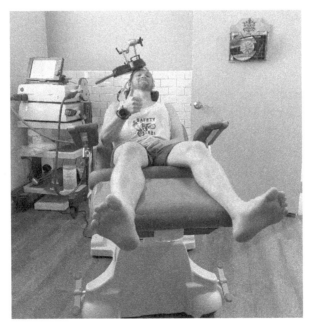

Healing my nervous system with transcranial magnetic stimulation, one of the many helpful modalities provided at Resiliency Brain Health in Dallas, Texas.

The following two weeks immersed me in various therapeutic approaches to address my TBI. Each day, I started with brain influencer Dr. Michelle Eisenmann guiding me through eye movement drills, using nothing more than a popsicle stick adorned with tiny stickers. Following the sticker with my eyes while keeping my head stationary quickly led to eye fatigue, requiring me to rest. As Michelle explained, the eyes were nothing more than an extension of the brain, and these exercises served to boost circulation and enhance brain function.

The TMS machine that initially mapped out my brain found another purpose as the days unfolded. Directing magnetic pulses toward both hemispheres of my frontal lobe acted as a pacifier for my nervous system. The switch flipped from the adrenaline-charged sympathetic system (fight or flight) to the calming parasympathetic system (rest and digest), leaving me with tranquil contentment. After just seven minutes under its influence, I felt the relaxation you'd expect from a couple of beers—without the debilitating side effects. It was a serenity reminiscent of Peter from *Office Space*, post-hypnosis.

Most days saw me engaged in simple exercises, like playing catch while balancing on one leg. The majority of the activities used equipment you'd find in a standard gym or elementary school art room. The real magic, however, was in the hands of the gifted physicians orchestrating the healing process. The exceptional team at Resiliency Brain Health had found the keys to healing, unveiling a synergistic combination of effective healing methods. Their holistic approach set them apart. They didn't focus on a singular aspect; they focused on the whole body, nervous system, and mind. They saw the bigger picture, breaking free from many mainstream physicians' pigeonholed mentality and capabilities. Their frustration with the pharmaceutical industry was palpable, considering the number of legitimately safe, effective treatments—treatments that could significantly reduce dependency on pharmaceutical drugs and drastically improve quality of life—being shunned.

After two weeks of intense therapy, it was time for a reevaluation. The improvements were staggering. I was calmer; my mind was more precise; my focus was sharper; my sleep quality had improved significantly. I hadn't felt this whole since before my ejection.

In hindsight, had these treatments been available when my TBI/PTS symptoms first emerged, I might still be in the cockpit of the Super Hornet. How much experience could have been retained across the military just in the members I had met within this small community of healing veterans had they received this kind of treatment early on? Many of these modalities could be utilized proactively to optimize performance and prolong careers.

*   *   *

Dr. Kirk Parsley, a former SEAL turned physician, has blazed trails in proactive, performance-based health care, originally for active-duty SEALs. When he returned to the navy as a physician, his team used comprehensive blood tests as a first step to address the underlying causes of operator syndrome, a condition common in the SEAL community. Operator syndrome is essentially the combination of physical injury to the brain or TBI and the resulting symptoms of PTS, which are undoubtedly interlinked.

Dr. Parsley is aware of the ubiquity of TBI within the SEAL community. This damage can occur from various factors, including exposure to explosions, gunfire, high g-forces, chronic stress, and numerous other hazards inherent to the profession.

It seems evident that the cumulative effects of repeated exposure to high g-forces and the stress experienced in the cockpit of fighter aircraft contribute to TBI/PTS in the same way as within the SEAL community. While these brain injuries can be detrimental over time, Dr. Parsley's work shows that their effects can be mitigated. The brain can recover.

His treatments, which involve a combination of nutraceuticals, peptides, testosterone replacement therapy, hyperbaric oxygen therapy, quality sleep, and other non-pharmaceutical remedies, have led to remarkable enhancements in his patients' physical and mental performances. He has observed accelerated healing rates and new peaks in performance levels.

Despite these promising results, his groundbreaking methods were met with resistance from navy leadership, who claimed he was overstepping his professional boundaries. This disapproval prevented him from utilizing the same techniques that consistently improved lives, ultimately leading to his exit from active duty. Ironically, SEAL Team Six later recruited him to continue offering these same effective treatments to the SEALs who face the most grueling deployment schedules and exposure to TBI within the community.

Dr. Parsley's approach to performance-based medicine should be a benchmark in military health care. It has showcased the potential for improved performance, reduced injuries, and increased retention, yielding significant benefits for military personnel and overall military readiness. With proactive interventions like these, we can prevent the loss of valuable personnel into whom millions of dollars have been invested for training.

I hope the Resiliency Brain Clinic's methods and Dr. Parsley's approach can be widely adopted, including in the strike-fighter community. Given that aircrew often suffer silently from operator syndrome, a small investment in what is poured into training each naval aviator in proactive, performance-based treatments could yield substantial dividends, much as it has for the SPECWAR community. We possess the tools to transform health care. It's time to use them.

* * *

The improvement I experienced due to these interventions was tangible.

I slept better, my physical performance improved, and my libido strengthened, something the psych meds had robbed me of. I started training five to six days a week for the Marji Gesick 100, the most brutal single-day mountain bike race on the planet. The hundred-and-some-mile route, featuring 12,500 feet of elevation gain over rugged, technical terrain, was a daunting prospect even for professional athletes. Fully weaned off quetiapine, I felt lighter, and my body began to regain its muscle tone. Having a challenging goal to work toward was immensely beneficial. Despite my injuries, I believed that if I could stick to my rigorous training plan, I might have a chance at completing the Marji. As I penned this book and made guest appearances on numerous podcasts, my story began resonating with those struggling with health-related battles. The messages of gratitude I received were uplifting, with some even crediting me for providing a beacon of hope that prevented them from taking their own lives. This healing journey had given me a renewed sense of purpose, and I felt compelled to share this newfound knowledge with countless others struggling in silence.

Cara was relieved to see the lasting changes in me, and over time, my family came to support my decision to step away from quetiapine. It's been years since I last set foot in a VA facility. Still, I sometimes wonder if the psychiatrists and psychologists

Appearing on the *MERGED* podcast with fellow F/A-18 pilot Ryan Graves.

who once insisted that I'd never survive without relying on quetiapine for the rest of my life might someday read my story or hear my voice on a podcast. Maybe then they'd understand the power of finding a different path to genuine healing.

CHAPTER 39

Upon returning from the TBI clinic, I recommitted to my Marji training plan, continued my supplement regimen, and maintained a diet rich in whole foods. Most days, I'd rise before the break of dawn, hopping onto my bike for hours-long training rides, prepping for the Marji mountain bike race. I navigated miles of winding single-track through the undulating terrain of Northern Michigan. The glow of my bike lights often caught the darting figures of whitetail deer, raccoons, and owls. On a few occasions, I narrowly missed colliding with a local porcupine. The woods teemed with life before the sun could peek over the horizon.

Life flowed smoothly, almost like I was in sync with a higher purpose. Perhaps the trials and tribulations I had experienced were a prerequisite to the person I was destined to be. I was on a trajectory of continual growth, and the more I helped others, the stronger I became. The gratification from witnessing others regain hope and triumph was so overwhelming that it often moved me to tears of joy.

As autumn painted the world in a riot of colors, my endurance capabilities peaked despite my residual injuries. I had been training alongside my longtime kiteboarding friend, Matt. We fed off each other's energy and determination. A few days before the Marji, we packed up and journeyed to Marquette,

Michigan, with our families in tow. It was time to put my year of training to the test in the most brutal mountain bike race ever conceived.

A long day still ahead of me on the brutal course of the Marji Gesick 100.

The predawn energy at the starting line was humming. A rock band set the rhythm of the morning as racers huddled around campfires. The guitarist unleashed a rendition of the national anthem a la Jimi Hendrix, the roar of Harley Davidson engines serving as a prelude. This was a race unlike any other I had experienced. The racers launched into a foot race around a short, wooded trail loop in what's known as a Le Mans start, designed to spread out the racers before entering the narrow trails on bikes. Once I was back on my bike, I maintained the sustainable pace to which I had trained. The swarm of riders was dense for the first thirty miles, leading to frustration as I walked behind riders who struggled with climbs I would usually easily conquer. A mental note was made—if I were ever to attempt this madness again, I'd go full throttle at the get-go to avoid the crowd.

As the morning wore on, I was amazed at how swiftly time passed. The initial sections of the race were relatively manageable until we reached a technical segment known as Pine Knob. Pine Knob presented a steep ascent and descent, its surface covered in sharp, loose rocks. Traction on what seemed like broken tile shards left riders on the edge of control. A punctured tire could quickly derail a rider. The consequences of minor mistakes rapidly launched riders tumbling down the jagged gradients. Many racers were already beginning to falter.

I managed to get through unscathed and soon emerged into a clearing teeming with spectators and volunteers, all eager to replenish the racers. Having ridden for several hours, I decided to take a short break to consume half a burrito I had packed. A group throwing a tailgate party handed me a chilled light beer. The icy liquid cooled me, offering the ideal hydration and caloric intake blend. At the very least, it served as a morale booster.

Gratefully thanking the lively group, I resumed my journey, fully aware that the day would only grow progressively more challenging. The forthcoming sections proved significantly more daunting, with steep inclines up narrow single-track trails carpeted with roots, rocks, and struggling bikers. Even when others occasionally overtook me, I maintained my steady pace, conscious of the common mistake of pushing too hard for too long in the early stages and burning out.

The heat and humidity intensified as the sun rose higher in the sky, compelling me to hydrate continuously. I was meticulous about my intake of electrolytes and food, adhering to the mantra that ultra-distance racing is an eating contest. Even when the thought of food was off-putting, I knew I had to keep consuming it. However, exceeding three hundred calories an hour could also prove detrimental. By midday, the miles of jarring, rough terrain were beginning to take a toll.

At this point, I was met by some friends running a support van near Mount Marquette, where I had been navigating up and down the expert-level trails. My body was starting to cramp, and a wave of nausea swept over me. My skin was a bright shade of red and was radiating heat. I downed extra water, half a peanut butter and jelly sandwich, and electrolyte tablets to fight off impending heat stroke. After exchanging high-fives with my support crew, I returned to the trails.

The Marji course felt like a relentless climb. It was. The ascents demanded constant focus and sporadic bursts of power well beyond a sustainable heart rate. Due to their technical nature, the descents were often more taxing than the climbs, particularly on the upper body. Around the sixty-mile mark, I found myself wrestling with self-doubt. Accumulating nausea, muscle spasms, and exhaustion compelled me to veer off the trail. I was bonking hard. Discarding my bike, I collapsed, feeling like complete dogshit.

Todd and Danny, the creators of the Marji, warn anyone considering such a ludicrous pursuit that the course will push them to their limits. I was at that precipice. I still had fifty miles of the most demanding biking ahead, but I was plagued with cramps and waves of nausea.

I took a moment to drink more water and massage my cramping legs. After about ten minutes, I felt like I could attempt to continue. Once back on the bike, every pedal push was a struggle as my weary legs labored to maintain a reasonable pace. I continued until I arrived at a clearing on one of the rare flat stretches of trail. There, a party scene was in full swing. Volunteers and spectators were grilling and offering a variety of snacks and drinks while enjoying the party themselves.

It was time to utilize the ultra-endurance athletes' secret weapon to avert bonking out: an ice-cold classic cola. Its combination of sugar, caffeine, and whatever magic the coca leaf offers has a reviving effect when used on rare occasions. Many seasoned ultra-endurance athletes swear by it. Some even carry watered-down cola in their hydration packs to sip on regularly during races. I, too, became a believer. My typical avoidance of soda and caffeine made the boost much more invigorating. I powered up like Popeye after guzzling a tin of spinach. As I left the trailside party, my legs felt revived, my nausea had subsided, and I was raring to take on the upcoming sections.

I was nearly seventy miles in when I reached the notorious RAMBA trails and a heavy rainstorm soaked the area. Although the downpour eased the grueling midafternoon heat, it made the already challenging RAMBA trails even more daunting. When dry, these trails had posed the most difficult riding I had ever experienced. Wet, the slippery rocks, roots, and muddy clay trails were barely navigable. Many more hike-a-bike sections awaited, and the downhill segments were set to be treacherously slippery.

The intense concentration required to navigate these challenging, chunky trails made the day seem to fly by. It was already late afternoon when I arrived at Jackson Mine Park in Negaunee, providing one of my last chances to resupply. I equipped my helmet and bar lights in anticipation of the looming darkness. Given the dark, wet conditions and my fatigue, the remainder of the course would likely take nearly twice as long to complete as it would under dry, daylight conditions with fresh legs. The brutal Marji course was designed to push riders to the point of them wanting to quit. Many gave up at Jackson Mine Park, daunted by the prospect of facing the worst part of the race in such challenging conditions. Seeing fit athletes sprawled on the ground, surrendering despite their fully capable bodies, paradoxically motivated me. The most demanding and most hazardous sections were still to come—in the dark, no less.

Whenever I thought I had conquered the most challenging climb or downhill, another even more treacherous section would emerge. Once a thriving mining town, Negaunee now felt like a ghost town. Deserted industrial buildings were being reclaimed by nature as the mines beneath them had collapsed. The place had a run-down air about it. The eerie screeches of wild animals echoed through the dense canopy of the dark, lonely woods. It was unsettling enough during the day with friends, but now, having not seen another rider for over an hour, I was winding through the endless darkness alone. Occasionally, I'd spot another headlight in the distance or the reflection of a skull and crossbones sign affixed to a tree, serving as a trail marker. The course required self-navigation, and the GPS on my cycling computer often lagged, making the sight of a "Blame Danny," "Blame Todd," or skull and crossbones trail marker a comforting confirmation that I was on the right course.

The nerve damage in my left leg was becoming increasingly troublesome. Focusing on not riding off the cliff's edge helped me ignore the sharp pain in my atrophied left foot. My aggravated foot drop became so weak that it was nearly impossible to unclip my left foot from the pedal. I started getting trapped in the pedals, causing me to crash onto my side.

My forearms felt like they'd been operating a jackhammer for over fifteen hours straight, making it difficult to hold onto the handlebars. The severed median nerve in my left forearm contributed to my increasingly weak grip, so I could no longer operate my dropper seat post. Squeezing the front brake was becoming a struggle. The slippery conditions made every rock and root feel like it was trying to slide my bike out from under me, and the narrow seat continued to chafe and irritate the blisters forming on my undercarriage.

After a long, lonesome, eerie grind, I returned to Jackson Mine Park for my final resupply. The festivities had long since ended, and other than the occasional sighting of a few other stubborn riders, it felt eerily barren. I laid down momentarily and questioned if I could physically get back up. I still had about twenty miles of the most challenging riding of the entire course. I drank another cola and ate a candy bar along with my more sustainable nutrition for a boost. The simple sugars were as much about boosting my morale as fueling my body. I had come this far. I was determined not to quit now.

Leaving the faint lighting of the park behind, I headed off into the unsettling darkness. My body was weary, but I felt a surge of energy as I overtook more exhausted riders. The race was beginning to resemble rock climbing with a bike more than an actual bike race. The trails were incredibly steep, and the damp, moss-covered rocks seemed determined to knock me onto my bruised ass. Some sections near the end were so sketchy that it was a challenge to climb them on foot.

My cycling computer read 103 miles when I passed a small group of struggling riders who were under the false impression that the finish line was close since we had already hit the one-hundred-mile mark. We still had at least ten more grueling miles ahead, which would only worsen. I knew Todd and Danny loved to add extra miles to the advertised distance to crush souls. If the struggling riders kept conquering one little section at a time, hoping it was the last, they might make it to the finish line.

At one point, the trail wound up the side of a cliff, a path that would have been difficult even for a mountain goat. At the top of the ridge was a massive boulder. Naturally, the trail required us to climb ultra-steep goat trails to reach the top. Halfway up, I passed another rider who had called it a night trailside, snoring peacefully. Once I finally reached the summit, my heart was pounding from the brutal ascent. I took a moment to sit and catch my breath next to a jovially drunk man handing out candy bars and slurred words of wisdom. Even at four in the morning, the positive Marji vibe was alive.

Pushing on, I made it to a paved road. I knew from pre-riding the section weeks prior that there was only one significant climb before the finish line. Despite my overwhelming fatigue and the flare-up of my ailments, I managed to ride up to the top of that final peak without stopping. Waiting at the top was a bucket of wooden coins. Throughout the race, we had to collect these tokens to prove that we had ridden the entire course. Missing even just one meant disqualification. The three wooden tokens I had collected throughout the course spelled out "Find," "Your," and "Limits." The final coin read "Finisher." I would be a finisher if I could descend the steep downhill stretch ahead without crashing.

Emerging into the small, deserted downtown area of pre-dawn Ishpeming, I spotted the finish line. Despite everything, I completed the final stretch with a powerful sprint thanks to a surge of adrenaline. One of the diehard volunteers checked my cycling computer and asked for my coins. He scrutinized them with his flashlight, then extended his hand with a smile to congratulate me. I was an official #Finisher.

The Marji had been every bit as grueling as people had said it would be and then some. I was filled with euphoria. I set down my bike and sat on the cold sidewalk, exhausted but victorious. Another finisher handed me a chilled beer. My grip was so shot that I had to use my teeth to open it. One sip was all my body could handle without puking. I had pushed myself well past my perceived limits, my mind showing my broken body what it was capable of despite so many ailments. After riding for over twenty-one hours straight and covering over 12,500 feet of elevation gain, I had completed 115 miles of the most punishing mountain biking imaginable. Not bad for a guy with a handicap plate.

EPILOGUE

The transformation in my life over the past two years has been remarkable. From a depressed, fragmented version of myself, I have reemerged as an ultra-endurance athlete, a motivational speaker, and a writer. Most importantly, I have reclaimed my roles as a devoted husband and father, roles that were nearly lost to the depths of severe mental illness. Healing is a continuing journey, and not every day is good, but the overall trajectory seems upward. The path to healing isn't linear, and I'm unsure if there's an endpoint. I feel a sense of alignment with the universe and a renewed mission to aid others in overcoming their life challenges. I want to spread the message that healing is possible despite what one might have been led to believe. It all starts with a spark of hope.

I am deeply grateful for all the love and support I've received throughout this journey. To all veterans who may be struggling, know that a growing network of nonprofit organizations is diligently working to address the substantial gaps in the VA health care system. Much of this healing can be accomplished through lifestyle changes, regardless of whether you are a veteran. Prioritizing sleep, nutrition, regular exercise, and connection to others and nature are powerful healing tools that don't cost much other than a change in habits.

At the end of this book, I have provided a list of all the organizations that have helped me in my recovery journey.

Top left: Inspiring others through motivational speaking.
Top right: Advocating for psychedelic-assisted therapy in Washington, DC, with the founder of the Heroic Hearts Project, Jesse Gould.
Bottom left: Michigan congressman Jack Bergman and I advocating for psychedelic-assisted therapy in Washington, DC.
Bottom right: Completing a marathon in London, England, during a wild adventure around the world with the 7x Project to help end veteran suicide.

"No tree can grow to heaven unless its roots reach down to hell."

—Carl Jung

Please tap into these resources and share them with anyone who is struggling. We can assist each other in getting back into the fight. We can be beacons of hope, lighting the path toward a new chapter in history. As more of us heal, we can shift our energies to help those who are still in the throes of their struggles. Together, we can play a significant role in healing our nation and world. But first, we must heal ourselves.

"Veterans are the light at the tip of the candle, illuminating the way for the whole nation. If veterans can achieve awareness, transformation, understanding, and peace, they can share the realities of war with the rest of society. And they can teach us how to make peace with ourselves and each other, so we never have to use violence to resolve conflicts again."

—Thich Nhat Hanh

In the meantime, if some rowdy extraterrestrials arrive with a scheme to enslave humanity, you'll find me at the front of the line, strapping a nuke onto a battered old Super Hornet and blasting in max afterburner straight into the mothership. For now, though, I plan to share my story as I strive to raise my wonderful little wildlings alongside my beautiful wife. Stay scrappy.

POSTSCRIPT

While not professionally certified in medicine, I've explored various healing modalities over the past decade. I am not prescribing any course of action, but I'm sharing what has helped me on my path toward achieving optimal health.

Fundamental Components of Health:

Hope | Sleep | Nutrition | Exercise | Connection | Antitoxin

Igniting hope and taking the first step is how you start your healing journey. The objective of this book is to shed light on the remarkable capacity of the human body, mind, and spirit to heal and rejuvenate. I hope it serves as a beacon of hope for someone out there. If you have a friend that may be struggling, reach out. You might be the spark of hope they need.

Sleep is a fundamental pillar of healing. I suggest reading *Why We Sleep* by Matthew Walker or listening to his podcasts for a thorough understanding of its importance. With Robert Sweetman's 62romeo sleep program specifically designed for veterans and first responders, you can acquire valuable insights and actionable steps to improve your sleep quality. Aim for seven and a half to eight hours of sleep each night as adults; anything less will gradually deteriorate your health and hinder the healing process.

Nutrition is vital to your body's functionality and healing process. A good starting point is Michael Pollan's book, *In Defense of Food*. His advice is simple yet powerful: Eat food. Not too much. Stick to whole foods, preferably organic, found around the grocery store's periphery. Avoid products with over seven ingredients, unpronounceable names, or numbers.

Additionally, limit or eradicate alcohol, added sugars, gluten, seed oils, and industrially produced meats. Switching to a healthier diet might require some relearning, but once you shift to real food, your body will start to crave it. Proper nutrition enhances physical well-being and can unlock positive epigenetics, allowing you to look and feel your best. Start with what you like; ensure it is real food.

Regular physical activity does not necessitate becoming an elite athlete. Discover an exercise you enjoy and make it part of your routine. Staying active doesn't require fancy equipment or expensive gym memberships. Simple exercises like planks, push-ups, squats, and lunges can be highly beneficial. Yoga can also be a great choice. And don't forget about mental exercise—meditation can do wonders for your mind and soul. The Wisdom Dojo offers an online meditation course worth checking out.

Building connections and being part of a community is critical to your well-being. This may come naturally for veterans during active service, but the risk of isolation grows post-service. Engaging in group activities or volunteering can be excellent ways to cultivate connections. We are social beings and thrive on meaningful interactions.

Additionally, connecting with nature is essential. Regular exposure to sunlight, fresh air, and the great outdoors is highly beneficial. The further we stray from nature, the sicker we become.

Avoiding toxins can significantly aid your body's healing process. Often sneaking into our lives in many forms, toxins can disrupt our bodies' proper functioning. Some common toxins include artificial food additives, glyphosate (found in most nonorganic produce), chlorinated or fluorinated water, regular and diet sodas, added sugars, seed oils, alcohol, gluten, nicotine, recreational drugs, and excessive caffeine. Minimizing exposure to social media, mainstream media, toxic people, and cellular radiation can help reduce inflammation and heal our bodies and minds.

Remember, health is a journey, not a destination. Sometimes, healing requires stillness. Taking small but consistent steps toward improvement can lead to a significant transformation over time. Hold yourself accountable and witness the ripple effect that one good decision can create. With determination and persistence, you'll be amazed at where this journey leads you.

RESOURCES

Here is a compilation of organizations that significantly contributed to my healing process. I express my deepest gratitude for their work and resources. They might offer the support you need, but if they don't, don't be disheartened. Kindness and support are abundant in the world; you only need the courage to seek them out. The real change comes in improving your habits, and that change comes from within yourself.

If you're interested in contributing to nonprofit organizations that are creating transformative impacts in the lives of veterans and first responders, supporting these organizations will do just that.

Operation Surf: Surf program that gets veterans and first responders to experience the healing power of the ocean. Run by big wave surfing legend Van Curaza. https://operationsurf.org/

Wake for Warriors: Marine attack helicopter pilot Dave Deep will get you out shredding behind the most capable wake surfing boats on the planet along with legends like Shaun Murray, Jodi Grassman, and Rusty Malinoski. https://www.wakefor-warriors.org/

Heroic Hearts Project: Former US Army Ranger Jesse Gould helps combat veterans gain access to indigenous medicines and provides the crucial resources for preparing and then integrating post-journey. https://www.heroicheartsproject.org/ and https://soltara.co/

Defenders of Freedom: Founded by Donna Cranston to help veterans heal from TBI. The organization funds recipients to attend two weeks of transformative healing modalities at Resiliency Brain Health with Dr. Scharlene Gaudet and Dr. Michelle Eisenmann. You can check out @thebrainfluencer on Instagram for helpful tips on healing the brain. https://www.defendersoffreedom.us/ and https://www.resiliencybh.com/

62romeo: Groundbreaking sleep program designed by former SEAL turned sleep genius Robert Sweetman. https://www.sleepgeni.us/

OpenWater: Pro surfer Danny Nichols teamed up with army combat veteran Kyle Kelly to help veterans and first responders reconnect by completing breathtaking open ocean crossings. https://www.operationopenwater.org/

The Wisdom Dojo: Learn to meditate with master meditation coach Bill Filter and his cofounder, former US Air Force F-15 combat pilot Mark Williams. Their caring staff, comprised of former military Special Forces and tactical aviators, may give you a new perspective on meditation. The Wisdom Dojo offers an online video series, meditation training, and retreats. https://thewisdomdojo.org/

Veterans Exploring Treatment Solutions (VETS): Founded by former SEAL Marcus Capone and his steadfast wife, Amber Capone, on a mission to end veteran suicide. VETS provides veterans access to psychedelic-assisted therapy. https://vetsolutions.org/

No Fallen Heroes Foundation: Former US Navy F-18 pilot Matthew "Whiz" Buckley helps veterans, first responders, and their families heal from trauma by providing resources, education, and access to psychedelic-assisted therapy. https://nofallenheroesfoundation.org/ and https://www.awakenyoursoul.co/

Birds Eye View Project: Founded by former Navy SEAL Ryan "Birdman" Parrott, the Birds Eye View Project raises funds to help various initiatives that help those in need. https://birdseyeviewproject.org/

Root and Wisdom: Authentic indigenous medicine retreats in Costa Rica. https://rootandwisdom.com/

Soltara Healing Centers: Transformative psychedelic-assisted therapy in both Costa Rica and Peru. https://soltara.co/

Awaken Your Soul: Authentic ceremonial experience with the most powerful indigenous medicine, iboga, in the heart of the Costa Rican jungle. https://www.awakenyoursoul.co/

This is just a handful of resources. Countless more organizations are out there, able to help those in need. The first step is asking for help. If you need help taking the first step and don't know where to start, please get in touch with me. You are not alone in this fight.

www.KeganGill.com
LinkedIn: Kegan Gill
Instagram: @KeganSmurfGill

ACKNOWLEDGMENTS

I wouldn't be here today without the overwhelming support and love I received throughout my recovery journey.

To my incredible wife, Cara: You have endured more challenges in the past eight years than most people face in a lifetime. Your resilience, patience, and love carried me through my darkest moments. I couldn't have made it without you. I love you deeply.

To my two sweet little wildlings: You reignited my spirit during my darkest times, even when I struggled to show it. You gave me the strength to keep going, and I love you both more than words can express.

To my parents: I can't imagine the heartbreak you endured seeing me unconscious, bruised, and broken in the ICU. You faced even more pain, watching me slip into psychosis again and again. Through it all, you stood by me. Your unwavering support gave me the foundation I needed to heal.

To my in-laws, Jeff and Kelly Killian: Thank you for your unwavering support during our most challenging times. Your love and dedication to Cara and our children provided a sanctuary that helped save our family. I am eternally grateful for the strength and stability you offered when we needed it most.

Thank you, Diego, Fisty, Bish, Kelvin, Sparkles, AC1 Hercules, Cheech, Joey, HS-11, HSC-28, the nearby fishing crew, the US Coast Guard, and all the saviors who helped recover me from the ocean.

To the Pukin' Dogs, the bitches in heat, to the mighty Rhino, and the single-seat: Fighters forever. Attack when we must. Here's to the new guy—don't fuck it up! Thank you, Diego, Flopper, Anoya, Yoyo, Yak, Beav, Smuggla, Cawk, Scribe, Dick Vampire, Sugar, Barf, Gump, Hipster, Marley, McLovin, Fisty, Dr. Ape, Lewick, Bits, Poop, and the three-hundred-plus hardworking, enlisted members of Strike Fighter Squadron One-Four-Three.

To the surgical dream team at Sentara Norfolk General Hospital's emergency department: Thank you for putting Humpty Dumpty back together again. Your skilled hands gave me a second chance.

To the Portsmouth Naval Hospital corpsmen and nursing staff: Thank you for your compassion and care throughout my recovery.

To the dedicated staff at the Hunter Holmes McGuire VA Polytrauma Center: Your persistence helped me regain my strength and get back on my feet.

To Kevin "Shaka" Chlan: Thank you for blazing the path back to the cockpit after your high-speed ejection and inspiring me to do the same.

To Dr. Christopher Hogan: Thank you for restoring my dexterity and function, allowing me to play the piano again and operate the Super Hornet controls with my left hand. You advised against rock climbing, so I took up jujitsu instead. So far, so good!

Thank you, Vice Admiral Mike Shoemaker and the FNAEB board members, for allowing me to saddle back up on the fire-breathing dragon that bucked me off.

Thank you, Amanda "Aunt Smuggs" Johnson, for kicking my ass back into shape.

Thank you, Stephanie Perez and the Oceana Physical Therapy Clinic staff.

Thank you to Dr. Pike, Dr. Duarte, and all the flight docs who helped me obtain a miraculous stack of medical waivers to return to the cockpit.

Thank you to the VFA-106 Gladiator instructors who helped me return to the cockpit.

To Tommy "Fisty" Flynn, Vinny "Leroy" Coleman, Neal "Shakey" Dunne, Aaron "Spicoli" Thurber, Rich "Beaker" Tiberio, Tom "Nuker" Kilcline, Greg "Catman" Linderman, Ian Sciford, Pat Romero, and Brian Anderson: Thank you for your friendship during my recovery. You guys saved me by getting me back in the ocean.

Thank you, Leo Perez, for inspiring me to heal through woodworking.

Thank you to the VFA-136 Knighthawks, Whep, Blue, Choda Boy, Cougar, Radio, Squeezer, Blart, Spider Monkey, Blonders, Sadness, Sid, Quitter, DPOD, Sewer Pickle, FNGs, OPSEC Eagle, SWO Face, Joey, Gunner, Skillet, and the hundreds of dedicated, enlisted members of Strike Fighter Squadron One-Three-Six.

To Dr. Robert Eberly, Dr. Michelle Rose, and the NAS Lemoore medical staff: Thank you for helping me navigate the bureaucratic nightmare of the medical board process.

To Van Curaza and the Operation Surf crew: Thank you for reconnecting me to the healing power of the ocean during my darkest times.

To Matt Myers: Your friendship and inspiration helped lead me to a healthier lifestyle. Thank you for always being there.

To Dave Deep, Shawn Murray, Rusty Malinoski, Jodi Grassman, Tyler Densford, Stefan LeRoy, Bill, and the members of Wake for Warriors: Thank you for helping spread the shred and building such an incredible community.

To Mike, Dr. Kirby, and the Battle Creek inpatient psych facility staff: Your dedication to improving the lives of veterans during their darkest moments will never be forgotten.

To Marcus and Amber Capone of Vet Solutions: Thank you for raising awareness and destigmatizing psychedelic-assisted therapy for veterans like me who battle PTSD and TBI.

To Adam and Andrew Marr of the Warrior Angels Foundation: Thank you for welcoming me into a community of extraordinary veterans and giving me access to healing when I thought there were no other options.

To Chief Phil Lane Jr.: Your guidance in our indigenous ceremony helped me rediscover my purpose.

To Vance McMurray: Thank you for pushing me to find the ultra-endurance wolf within.

To Dr. Michael Lewis: Your wisdom and expertise were invaluable during the early stages of my brain healing.

To Dr. Mark Gordon: Thank you for your insights, products, and work in exposing the truth behind healing PTSD and TBI.

To Chris Palmitessa: Thank you for inviting me to record my first podcast.

To Kelsi Sheren: You gave me the courage to share my story. Thank you.

To Jesse Gould: Your generosity through the Heroic Hearts Project was life-changing for me and has drastically improved the lives of 1,500-plus other veterans and military spouses.

To the healers at La Medicina in Tarapoto, Peru: Your gifts helped me heal and transform beyond anything I could have imagined.

To Eric "Moose" Smith, Mark Williams, and Bill Filter of The Wisdom Dojo: Thank you for helping me build a life-changing meditation practice and connecting me with a family of outstanding veterans.

To Donna Cranston and the staff of Defenders of Freedom: Thank you for funding my healing at the Resiliency Brain Health Clinic. The talented Dr. Scharlene Gaudet, Dr. Michelle Eisenmann, and Jay played a significant role in my recovery.

To Aria Everts: Thank you for your spiritual guidance and helping heal my nervous system.

To Dr. Eleanor Womack and Clay Womack: Your generosity and the healing modalities provided by ATX Hyperbarics and Westlake Medical Arts in Austin provided me with vibrant, lasting health.

To Dr. Kirk Parsley: Thank you for fighting to provide military members access to functional medicine. I appreciate your guidance and support.

To Matthew "Whiz" Buckley and the team at No Fallen Heroes: Thank you for funding my life-changing retreat at Awaken Your Soul.

To Anthony, Amber, Troy, Jo, Maya, Brayan, Maviango, Joelle, Zaida, Pamala, and the Awaken Your Soul staff: Thank you for your love and support on my healing journey.

To Troy Valencia: Thank you for guiding me through thirty years of psychotherapy in a single night and helping me reconnect with my soul.

To Danny Nichols, Kyle Kelly, Whitney Erikson, Morgan Hoesterey, Jay Wild, and all the Rusty Anchors at OpenWater: Thank you for the training and incredible paddling adventure from Catalina Island to the California coast.

To Robert Sweetman: Thank you for guiding me to restful sleep through your work with the 62romeo nonprofit.

To Ryan "Birdman" Parrott and the 7x Project crew: Thank you for giving me the adventure of a lifetime.

To Vinny Coleman and Garrett Jerde: Thank you for connecting me to the 7x Project and fundraising to make it happen.

To Chris Hauth, Jesse Itzler, Danny Pritchard, and Alex Racey: Thank you for helping launch my speaking career.

To Ernie Colling, Brendan Quisenberry, and the Transcend Foundation: Thank you for providing access to health optimization modalities that keep me functioning physically and mentally at my best.

To Corey Gillespie, Pat Burroughs, and the Armed Forces Shootout crew: Thank you for your ongoing camaraderie.

To Matt Helm and Larissa Czucnowsky for helping Cara and I salvage our marriage from the ashes.

To Kevin Shoults and Justin Sheehan of Seung-Ni Martial Arts: Thank you for helping me connect to my inner warrior.

To Tyler Carroll and Keith Dow of Dead Reckoning Collective: Thank you for your pre-publication advice.

To Bryce Hansen: Thank you for lending your incredible artistic talent to the cover design of this book. Your vision brought the story to life in a way that words alone could not capture.

To Austin Rowlader and Janessa Boulay: Thank you for your guidance in the early edits of this book.

To Andy Symonds, Journey Mathewson, Kayleigh Rucinski, Camma Duhamell, Holly Gorman, Fabiana Beuses, and the Ballast Books team: Thank you for turning my manuscript into a published book.

And finally, thank you to all the other kind souls who helped me along the way. Your support made this journey possible.

www.ingramcontent.com/pod-product-compliance
Lightning Source LLC
LaVergne TN
LVHW042040140125
801239LV00025B/589/J